AIR FRYER

Cookbook

with Color Pictures

For Beginners

365 Days Healthy, Fresh and
Foolproof Air Fryer Recipes for
Smart People on a Budget incl.
Tasty Desserts Special

Enoch Watsica

Table of Contents

Chapter 3 Beef, Pork, and Lamb

Chapter 4 Fish and Seafood

Chapter 5 Desserts

Chapter 6 Snacks and Appetizers

Appendix 1 Measurement Conversion Chart

Appendix 2 Air Fryer Cooking Chart

INTRODUCTION

I still remember the first recipe I tried. It was an easy air fryer potato wedges, and ever since then, I just couldn't stop.

Most people think french fries are the only thing to cook in an air fryer but you will be amazed at the amount of food magic one can make with an air fryer.

From bagels to chicken and even hard boiled eggs, you can get to have all the yummy treats you desire without having to count calories.

Not only does it make most unhealthy food healthy, an air fryer has so many uses that ,if allowed, can almost replace your oven!

We understand that a lot of people want to join the "air fryer gang" but don't know where to start from, or what to start with. This is why, in this first page, you need to know everything to help you decide if getting an air fryer is worth your investment.

Chapter 1 : A First-Timer's Guide to Air Fryer

Chapter 1 : A First-Timer's Guide to Air Fryer

What Is an Air Fryer?

An air fryer is a countertop convection oven that is designed to simulate deep frying. It has a fan and exhaust system that blows hot air and provides crispy frying flavor and evenly cooks and browns food without oil or fat.

It's convenient and super easy to use, and you can cook food in less time. Unlike an oven, it preheats quickly and can be versatile. For more advanced air fryers, you can get different functional buttons like fry,toast, bagel, etc, giving you tons of options to experiment with.

There are different criteria to consider when buying an air fryer, such as capacity, complexity, size, etc. It largely depends on what your budget is and what you plan to do with your air fryer.

Although there are loads of air fryer brands to choose from,there are just two major types of air fryers - Basket type and Oven type.

Basket Type

The basket type is the more popular one and it has a kind of wide drawer like compartment that serves as the basket in which food is cooked.

It comes in two different sizes, the small and the large. The small size ranges from 2.7 quarts to 3.7 quarts while the large sizes are between 4 quarts to 7 quarts.

The baskets also come in just two shapes. If it isn't round shaped, then it's square shaped.

Oven Type

Don't get confused! The air fryer oven is clearly different from a normal oven that has an air fryer function. They look more like a microwave or even a toaster oven, and instead of a basket, it has racks like a regular oven. Most air fryer ovens even come with a rotisserie chicken rod.

If compared, the basket style air fryer seems to cook a little bit faster than the air fryer oven.

How Do the Air Fryers Work?

Air fryers have inbuilt fan(s) that circulate hot air to cook food in a deep fry style, but without having to submerge it in oil.

The cooking chamber of the air fryer generates radiant heat from the heating element above the food and convective heat from a strong air stream flowing upward from the open bottom of the food chamber, providing heat from all sides. Small volumes of hot air are forced to pass over the surface of the heater and over the food, with no idle air circulation as in a convection oven. Then, a molded guide directs the airflow to the bottom of the food. In layman's terms, the air fryer has a fan and heating mechanism that blows hot air from the top and bottom compartments and around the cooking basket or tray.

The rapid air flow creates a frying effect that cooks and browns food evenly. In addition, the heat greatly reduces cooking time while keeping the food tender on the inside and crispy on the outside.

Typically, most air fryers have built-in temperature and timer adjustments for more precise cooking. Food is cooked in a basket/rack on a drip tray so that the heat can pass through and cook all sides of the food.

Some air fryers also come with simple preset cooking modes for fish, steak, chicken, cake, shrimp, meat and fries.

Now that we all understand these, below are important tips that can make cooking with an air fryer even more easier!

Important Tips to Keep in Mind

●Never forget the grate in the basket

Using the grate allows hot air to go round the food and keeps the food from sitting in excess oil.

●Check the condition of the food frequently

During the cooking process, always remember to pull out the basket to see how it is doing. To properly brown the food, take the basket out every one to two minutes. There is no need to turn off the machine because it will automatically shut off when the basket is removed.

●Be careful!

One of the benefits of using an air fryer is that the food cooks faster than you think. Although air fryers usually have cooking time and temperature manuals for different foods, you need to start with the lowest possible time and continue to increase the cooking time until you achieve the desired result.

Also, the less food you have in the basket, the shorter the cooking time. The more food you have, the longer it will take.

●Preheat your air fryer

Although not absolutely necessary, it will reduce your cooking time. Usually, this shouldn't take much time, about two to three minutes, so you can turn your air fryer on just before you're ready to start cooking.

●Never overcrowd your air fryer basket

Overcrowding your air fryer basket is usually a bad idea. When you put too much in your air fryer basket, your food is likely to steam instead of air fry, leaving you with soggy food. The best you can do is to split and air fry your food in batches. It may take longer but you will definitely love the result.

●Use foil

Having to clean up after every use can seem like a daunting task to many. To reduce the stress, you can line the bottom of your air fryer's basket with foil or parchment paper so that you'll have less to worry about cleanup. This is especially useful when you're cooking something that has plenty of sauce or spices which would otherwise drip and fly around the machine. Just make sure the food you're cooking has enough weight to hold down the paper or foil so that it doesn't fly around in the machine once you turn it on.

●Drippings = extra flavor

Remember the drippings that gathered at the bottom of your air fryer when you prepared greasy food? Yes, that one!

You do not have to throw it away because those drippings are full of flavor, so they can be used to make gravies, sauces, or even marinades. Make sure to save those drippings so you can use them to make your next meal even more delicious.

●Use heat-resistant materials only

Keeping your air fryer away from anything that easily burns or melts and placing it near materials that are heat-resistant are absolutely necessary ideas to adhere to.

The surface top must be heat- resistant, like a marble countertop. Make sure the vent isn't blowing onto anything that can burn or melt, like plastic.

●Always Refer To Your Manual

Air fryers are made by different manufacturers. Reading your manual will help you know and understand your individual gadget better.

How to Clean an Air Fryer In 7 Easy Steps

Step 1: Know what you need

You will need:

♦ A nonabrasive sponge
♦ Microfiber cloths
♦ A soft-bristle scrub brush
♦ Paper towels
♦ Dish soap
♦ Baking soda

Step 2: Make Sure Your Air Fryer Cool Down

It should have been unplugged and cooled down for at least 30 minutes. Once cooled, take out all of the removable parts of the appliance (basket, tray, pan).

Step 3: Clean the Removable Parts

Wash removable parts in warm soapy water. If the dishwasher is dishwasher-safe, put them in. If you have a lingering odor in your air fryer, clean the crevices with a wooden skewer, toothpick, or even an old toothbrush to knock off any stuck food. These hidden crumbs can burn over time, causing the machine to smoke and stink. In addition, if the food emits a strong odor while cooking, the smell may linger in your air fryer for a longer period of time, even after cleaning. To get rid of it, soak food baskets and drawers in soapy water for 30 to 60 minutes before cleaning again. If the odor persists, cut a lemon in half, rub it on the food baskets and drawers, wait 30 minutes, and then rinse again.

Use baking soda and water to make a cleaning paste to clean any hard-to-clean parts of the fryer or super-stubborn food residue that won't come off.

Step 4: Clean the Interior

Use a damp microfiber cloth or nonabrasive sponge with a splash of dish soap on it to wipe the interior of your air fryer. Then wipe again with a clean damp cloth to clean off any soap residue.

Step 5: Check the Heating Panel

Turn your air fryer upside-down and use a damp cloth or nonabrasive sponge to wipe down the heating element.

Step 6: Clean the Exterior

Wipe down the exterior using a cloth or sponge with a bit of dish soap, and then wipe away any residual soap with a clean damp cloth. Then wipe the outside with a paper towel.

Step 7: Reassemble Your Air Fryer

Finally, check to make sure every part of your air fryer is thoroughly dry. Reassemble all the removable parts into the main unit and boom! Your air fryer is as good as never used.

Chapter 2 Poultry

Chicken Schnitzel

Prep time: 15 minutes | Cook time: 5 minutes | Serves 4

½ cup all-purpose flour
1 teaspoon marjoram
½ teaspoon thyme
1 teaspoon dried parsley flakes
½ teaspoon salt
1 egg

1 teaspoon lemon juice
1 teaspoon water
1 cup breadcrumbs
4 chicken tenders, pounded thin, cut in half lengthwise
Cooking spray

Preheat the air fryer to 390ºF (199ºC) and spritz with cooking spray. 2. Combine the flour, marjoram, thyme, parsley, and salt in a shallow dish. Stir to mix well. 3. Whisk the egg with lemon juice and water in a large bowl. Pour the breadcrumbs in a separate shallow dish. 4. Roll the chicken halves in the flour mixture first, then in the egg mixture, and then roll over the breadcrumbs to coat well. Shake the excess off. 5. Arrange the chicken halves in the preheated air fryer and spritz with cooking spray on both sides. 6. Air fry for 5 minutes or until the chicken halves are golden brown and crispy. Flip the halves halfway through. 7. Serve immediately.

Garlic Soy Chicken Thighs

Prep time: 10 minutes | Cook time: 30 minutes |
Serves 1 to 2

2 tablespoons chicken stock
2 tablespoons reduced-sodium soy sauce
1½ tablespoons sugar
4 garlic cloves, smashed and peeled

2 large scallions, cut into 2- to 3-inch batons, plus more, thinly sliced, for garnish
2 bone-in, skin-on chicken thighs (7 to 8 ounces / 198 to 227 g each)

1. Preheat the air fryer to 375ºF (191ºC). 2. In a metal cake pan, combine the chicken stock, soy sauce, and sugar and stir until the sugar dissolves. Add the garlic cloves, scallions, and chicken thighs, turning the thighs to coat them in the marinade, then resting them skin-side up. Place the pan in the air fryer and bake, flipping the thighs every 5 minutes after the first 10 minutes, until the chicken is cooked through and the marinade is reduced to a sticky glaze over the chicken, about 30 minutes. 3. Remove the pan from the air fryer and serve the chicken thighs warm, with any remaining glaze spooned over top and sprinkled with more sliced scallions.

African Merguez Meatballs

Prep time: 30 minutes | Cook time: 10 minutes | Serves 4

1 pound (454 g) ground chicken	1 teaspoon ground cumin
2 garlic cloves, finely minced	½ teaspoon black pepper
1 tablespoon sweet Hungarian paprika	½ teaspoon ground fennel
	½ teaspoon ground coriander
1 teaspoon kosher salt	½ teaspoon cayenne pepper
1 teaspoon sugar	¼ teaspoon ground allspice

1. In a large bowl, gently mix the chicken, garlic, paprika, salt, sugar, cumin, black pepper, fennel, coriander, cayenne, and allspice until all the ingredients are incorporated. Let stand for 30 minutes at room temperature, or cover and refrigerate for up to 24 hours. 2. Form the mixture into 16 meatballs. Arrange them in a single layer in the air fryer basket. Set the air fryer to 400ºF (204ºC) for 10 minutes, turning the meatballs halfway through the cooking time. Use a meat thermometer to ensure the meatballs have reached an internal temperature of 165ºF (74ºC).

Buffalo Chicken Cheese Sticks

Prep time: 5 minutes | Cook time: 8 minutes | Serves 2

1 cup shredded cooked chicken	cheese
¼ cup buffalo sauce	1 large egg
1 cup shredded Mozzarella	¼ cup crumbled feta

1. In a large bowl, mix all ingredients except the feta. Cut a piece of parchment to fit your air fryer basket and press the mixture into a ½-inch-thick circle. 2. Sprinkle the mixture with feta and place into the air fryer basket. 3. Adjust the temperature to 400ºF (204ºC) and air fry for 8 minutes. 4. After 5 minutes, flip over the cheese mixture. 5. Allow to cool 5 minutes before cutting into sticks. Serve warm.

Nacho Chicken Fries

Prep time: 20 minutes | Cook time: 6 to 7 minutes per batch | Serves 4 to 6

1 pound (454 g) chicken tenders
Salt, to taste
¼ cup flour
2 eggs
¾ cup panko bread crumbs
¾ cup crushed organic nacho cheese tortilla chips
Oil for misting or cooking spray
Seasoning Mix:
1 tablespoon chili powder
1 teaspoon ground cumin
½ teaspoon garlic powder
½ teaspoon onion powder

Stir together all seasonings in a small cup and set aside. 2. Cut chicken tenders in half crosswise, then cut into strips no wider than about ½ inch. 3. Preheat the air fryer to 390ºF (199ºC). 4. Salt chicken to taste. Place strips in large bowl and sprinkle with 1 tablespoon of the seasoning mix. Stir well to distribute seasonings. 5. Add flour to chicken and stir well to coat all sides. 6. Beat eggs together in a shallow dish. 7. In a second shallow dish, combine the panko, crushed chips, and the remaining 2 teaspoons of seasoning mix. 8. Dip chicken strips in eggs, then roll in crumbs. Mist with oil or cooking spray. 9. Chicken strips will cook best if done in two batches. They can be crowded and overlapping a little but not stacked in double or triple layers. 10. Cook for 4 minutes. Shake basket, mist with oil, and cook 2 to 3 more minutes, until chicken juices run clear and outside is crispy. 11. Repeat step 10 to cook remaining chicken fries.

Brazilian Tempero Baiano Chicken Drumsticks

Prep time: 30 minutes | Cook time: 20 minutes | Serves 4

1 teaspoon cumin seeds
1 teaspoon dried oregano
1 teaspoon dried parsley
1 teaspoon ground turmeric
½ teaspoon coriander seeds
1 teaspoon kosher salt
½ teaspoon black peppercorns
½ teaspoon cayenne pepper
¼ cup fresh lime juice
2 tablespoons olive oil
1½ pounds (680 g) chicken drumsticks

1. In a clean coffee grinder or spice mill, combine the cumin, oregano, parsley, turmeric, coriander seeds, salt, peppercorns, and cayenne. Process until finely ground. 2. In a small bowl, combine the ground spices with the lime juice and oil. Place the chicken in a resealable plastic bag. Add the marinade, seal, and massage until the chicken is well coated. Marinate at room temperature for 30 minutes or in the refrigerator for up to 24 hours. 3. When you are ready to cook, place the drumsticks skin side up in the air fryer basket. Set the air fryer to 400ºF (204ºC) for 20 to 25 minutes, turning the legs halfway through the cooking time. Use a meat thermometer to ensure that the chicken has reached an internal temperature of 165ºF (74ºC). 4. Serve with plenty of napkins.

Tomatoes and Cheese Stuffed Chicken

Prep time: 15 minutes | Cook time: 20 minutes | Serves 4

2 ounces (57 g) cream cheese, softened
1 cup chopped tomatoes, sliced
½ cup shredded sharp Cheddar cheese
4 (6-ounce / 170-g) boneless, skinless chicken breasts
4 sliced hams
2 tablespoons mayonnaise
¼ teaspoon salt
¼ teaspoon garlic powder
⅛ teaspoon ground black pepper

1. In a medium bowl, combine cream cheese, tomato, ham, and Cheddar. Cut a 4-inch pocket into each chicken breast. Evenly divide mixture between chicken breasts; stuff the pocket of each chicken breast with the mixture. 2. Spread ¼ tablespoon mayonnaise per side of each chicken breast, then sprinkle both sides of breasts with salt, garlic powder, and pepper. 3. Place stuffed chicken breasts into ungreased air fryer basket so that the open seams face up. Adjust the temperature to 350ºF (177ºC) and air fry for 20 minutes, turning chicken halfway through cooking. When done, chicken will be golden and have an internal temperature of at least 165ºF (74ºC). Serve warm.

Lemon Thyme Roasted Chicken

Prep time: 10 minutes | Cook time: 60 minutes | Serves 6

1 (4-pound / 1.8-kg) chicken
2 teaspoons dried thyme
1 teaspoon garlic powder
½ teaspoon onion powder
2 teaspoons dried parsley
1 teaspoon baking powder
1 medium lemon
2 tablespoons salted butter, melted

1. Rub chicken with thyme, garlic powder, onion powder, parsley, and baking powder. 2. Slice lemon and place four slices on top of chicken, breast side up, and secure with toothpicks. Place remaining slices inside of the chicken. 3. Place entire chicken into the air fryer basket, breast side down. 4. Adjust the temperature to 350ºF (177ºC) and air fry for 60 minutes. 5. After 30 minutes, flip chicken so breast side is up. 6. When done, internal temperature should be 165ºF (74ºC) and the skin golden and crispy. To serve, pour melted butter over entire chicken.

Buttermilk-Fried Drumsticks

Prep time: 10 minutes | Cook time: 25 minutes | Serves 2

1 egg
½ cup buttermilk
¾ cup self-rising flour
¾ cup seasoned panko bread crumbs

1 teaspoon salt
¼ teaspoon ground black pepper (to mix into coating)
4 chicken drumsticks, skin on
Oil for misting or cooking spray

1. Beat together egg and buttermilk in shallow dish. 2. In a second shallow dish, combine the flour, panko crumbs, salt, and pepper. 3. Sprinkle chicken legs with additional salt and pepper to taste. 4. Dip legs in buttermilk mixture, then roll in panko mixture, pressing in crumbs to make coating stick. Mist with oil or cooking spray. 5. Spray the air fryer basket with cooking spray. 6. Cook drumsticks at 360ºF (182ºC) for 10 minutes. Turn pieces over and cook an additional 10 minutes. 7. Turn pieces to check for browning. If you have any white spots that haven't begun to brown, spritz them with oil or cooking spray. Continue cooking for 5 more minutes or until crust is golden brown and juices run clear. Larger, meatier drumsticks will take longer to cook than small ones.

Spicy Chicken Thighs and Gold Potatoes

Prep time: 5 minutes | Cook time: 25 minutes | Serves 4

4 bone-in, skin-on chicken thighs
½ teaspoon kosher salt or ¼ teaspoon fine salt
2 tablespoons melted unsalted butter
2 teaspoons Worcestershire sauce
2 teaspoons curry powder
1 teaspoon dried oregano leaves

½ teaspoon dry mustard
½ teaspoon granulated garlic
¼ teaspoon paprika
¼ teaspoon hot pepper sauce
Serve(optional):
4 medium Yukon gold potatoes, chopped
1 tablespoon extra-virgin olive oil

1. Sprinkle the chicken thighs on both sides with salt. 2. In a medium bowl, stir together the melted butter, Worcestershire sauce, curry powder, oregano, dry mustard, granulated garlic, paprika, and hot pepper sauce. Add the thighs to the sauce and stir to coat. 3. Insert the crisper plate into the basket and the basket into the unit. Preheat the unit by selecting AIR FRY, setting the temperature to 400ºF (204ºC), and setting the time to 3 minutes. Select START/STOP to begin. 4. Once the unit is preheated, spray the crisper plate with cooking oil. In the basket, combine the potatoes and olive oil and toss to coat. 5. Add the wire rack to the air fryer and place the chicken thighs on top. 6. Select AIR FRY, set the temperature to 400ºF (204ºC), and set the time to 25 minutes. Select START/STOP to begin. 7. After 19 minutes check the chicken thighs. If a food thermometer inserted into the chicken registers 165ºF (74ºC), transfer them to a clean plate, and cover with aluminum foil to keep warm. If they aren't cooked to 165ºF (74ºC), resume cooking for another 1 to 2 minutes until they are done. Remove them from the unit along with the rack. 8. Remove the basket and shake it to distribute the potatoes. Reinsert the basket to resume cooking for 3 to 6 minutes, or until the potatoes are crisp and golden brown. 9. When the cooking is complete, serve the chicken with the potatoes.

Broccoli Cheese Chicken

Prep time: 10 minutes | Cook time: 19 to 24 minutes | Serves 6

1 tablespoon avocado oil
¼ cup chopped onion
½ cup finely chopped broccoli
4 ounces (113 g) cream cheese, at room temperature
2 ounces (57 g) Cheddar cheese, shredded
1 teaspoon garlic powder
½ teaspoon sea salt, plus

additional for seasoning, divided
¼ freshly ground black pepper, plus additional for seasoning, divided
2 pounds (907 g) boneless, skinless chicken breasts
1 teaspoon smoked paprika

1. Heat a medium skillet over medium-high heat and pour in the avocado oil. Add the onion and broccoli and cook, stirring occasionally, for 5 to 8 minutes, until the onion is tender. 2. Transfer to a large bowl and stir in the cream cheese, Cheddar cheese, and garlic powder, and season to taste with salt and pepper. 3. Hold a sharp knife parallel to the chicken breast and cut a long pocket into one side. Stuff the chicken pockets with the broccoli mixture, using toothpicks to secure the pockets around the filling. 4. In a small dish, combine the paprika, ½ teaspoon salt, and ¼ teaspoon pepper. Sprinkle this over the outside of the chicken. 5. Set the air fryer to 400ºF (204ºC). Place the chicken in a single layer in the air fryer basket, cooking in batches if necessary, and cook for 14 to 16 minutes, until an instant-read thermometer reads 160ºF (71ºC). Place the chicken on a plate and tent a piece of aluminum foil over the chicken. Allow to rest for 5 to 10 minutes before serving.
Per Servingcalorie: 287 | fat: 16g | protein: 32g | carbs: 1g | sugars: 0g | fiber: 0g | sodium: 291mg

Easy Turkey Tenderloin

Prep time: 20 minutes | Cook time: 30 minutes | Serves 4

Olive oil
½ teaspoon paprika
½ teaspoon garlic powder
½ teaspoon salt
½ teaspoon freshly ground

black pepper
Pinch cayenne pepper
1½ pounds (680 g) turkey breast tenderloin

1. Spray the air fryer basket lightly with olive oil. 2. In a small bowl, combine the paprika, garlic powder, salt, black pepper, and cayenne pepper. Rub the mixture all over the turkey. 3. Place the turkey in the air fryer basket and lightly spray with olive oil. 4. Air fry at 370ºF (188ºC) for 15 minutes. Flip the turkey over and lightly spray with olive oil. Air fry until the internal temperature reaches at least 170ºF (77ºC) for an additional 10 to 15 minutes. 5. Let the turkey rest for 10 minutes before slicing and serving.

Chicken Cordon Bleu

Prep time: 20 minutes | Cook time: 15 to 20 minutes
| Serves 4

4 small boneless, skinless
chicken breasts
Salt and pepper, to taste
4 slices deli ham
4 slices deli Swiss cheese (about
3 to 4 inches square)

2 tablespoons olive oil
2 teaspoons marjoram
¼ teaspoon paprika
Serve:
Letture
Tomato

1. Split each chicken breast horizontally almost in two, leaving one edge intact. 2. Lay breasts open flat and sprinkle with salt and pepper to taste. 3. Place a ham slice on top of each chicken breast. 4. Cut cheese slices in half and place one half atop each breast. Set aside remaining halves of cheese slices. 5. Roll up chicken breasts to enclose cheese and ham and secure with toothpicks. 6. Mix together the olive oil, marjoram, and paprika. Rub all over outsides of chicken breasts. 7. Place chicken in air fryer basket and air fry at 360ºF (182ºC) for 15 to 20 minutes, until well done and juices run clear. 8. Remove all toothpicks. To avoid burns, place chicken breasts on a plate to remove toothpicks, then immediately return them to the air fryer basket. 9. Place a half cheese slice on top of each chicken breast and cook for a minute or so just to melt cheese.

Smoky Chicken Leg Quarters

Prep time: 30 minutes | Cook time: 23 to 27 minutes
| Serves 6

½ cup avocado oil
2 teaspoons smoked paprika
1 teaspoon sea salt
1 teaspoon garlic powder
½ teaspoon dried rosemary

½ teaspoon dried thyme
½ teaspoon freshly ground
black pepper
2 pounds (907 g) bone-in, skin-
on chicken leg quarters

1. In a blender or small bowl, combine the avocado oil, smoked paprika, salt, garlic powder, rosemary, thyme, and black pepper. 2. Place the chicken in a shallow dish or large zip-top bag. Pour the marinade over the chicken, making sure all the legs are coated. Cover and marinate for at least 2 hours or overnight. 3. Place the chicken in a single layer in the air fryer basket, working in batches if necessary. Set the air fryer to 400ºF (204ºC) and air fry for 15 minutes. Flip the chicken legs, then reduce the temperature to 350ºF (177ºC). Cook for 8 to 12 minutes more, until an instant-read thermometer reads 160ºF (71ºC) when inserted into the thickest piece of chicken. 4. Allow to rest for 5 to 10 minutes before serving.

Chicken Nuggets

Prep time: 10 minutes | Cook time: 15 minutes | Serves 4

1 pound (454 g) ground chicken thighs
½ cup shredded Mozzarella cheese

1 large egg, whisked
½ teaspoon salt
¼ teaspoon dried oregano
¼ teaspoon garlic powder

1. In a large bowl, combine all ingredients. Form mixture into twenty nugget shapes, about 2 tablespoons each. 2. Place nuggets into ungreased air fryer basket, working in batches if needed. Adjust the temperature to 375ºF (191ºC) and air fry for 15 minutes, turning nuggets halfway through cooking. Let cool 5 minutes before serving.

Honey-Glazed Chicken Thighs

Prep time: 5 minutes | Cook time: 14 minutes | Serves 4

Oil, for spraying
4 chicken thighs
3 tablespoons soy sauce
1 tablespoon balsamic vinegar

2 teaspoons honey
2 teaspoons minced garlic
1 teaspoon ground ginger

1. Preheat the air fryer to 400ºF (204ºC). Line the air fryer basket with parchment and spray lightly with oil. 2. Place the chicken in the prepared basket. 3. Cook for 7 minutes, flip, and cook for another 7 minutes, or until the internal temperature reaches 165ºF (74ºC) and the juices run clear. 4. In a small saucepan, combine the soy sauce, balsamic vinegar, honey, garlic, and ginger and cook over low heat for 1 to 2 minutes, until warmed through. 5. Transfer the chicken to a serving plate and drizzle with the sauce just before serving.

Thai Curry Meatballs

Prep time: 10 minutes | Cook time: 10 minutes | Serves 4

1 pound (454 g) ground chicken	1 tablespoon fish sauce
¼ cup chopped fresh cilantro	2 garlic cloves, minced
1 teaspoon chopped fresh mint	2 teaspoons minced fresh ginger
1 tablespoon fresh lime juice	½ teaspoon kosher salt
1 tablespoon Thai red, green, or	½ teaspoon black pepper
yellow curry paste	¼ teaspoon red pepper flakes

1. Preheat the air fryer to 400°F (204°C). 2. In a large bowl, gently mix the ground chicken, cilantro, mint, lime juice, curry paste, fish sauce, garlic, ginger, salt, black pepper, and red pepper flakes until thoroughly combined. 3. Form the mixture into 16 meatballs. Place the meatballs in a single layer in the air fryer basket. Air fry for 10 minutes, turning the meatballs halfway through the cooking time. Use a meat thermometer to ensure the meatballs have reached an internal temperature of 165°F (74°C). Serve immediately.

Porchetta-Style Chicken Breasts

Prep time: 10 minutes | Cook time: 15 minutes | Serves 4

½ cup fresh parsley leaves	1 teaspoon ground fennel
¼ cup roughly chopped fresh	½ teaspoon red pepper flakes
chives	4 (4-ounce / 113-g) boneless,
4 cloves garlic, peeled	skinless chicken breasts,
2 tablespoons lemon juice	pounded to ¼ inch thick
3 teaspoons fine sea salt	8 slices bacon
1 teaspoon dried rubbed sage	Sprigs of fresh rosemary, for
1 teaspoon fresh rosemary	garnish (optional)
leaves	

1. Spray the air fryer basket with avocado oil. Preheat the air fryer to 340°F (171°C). 2. Place the parsley, chives, garlic, lemon juice, salt, sage, rosemary, fennel, and red pepper flakes in a food processor and purée until a smooth paste forms. 3. Place the chicken breasts on a cutting board and rub the paste all over the tops. With a short end facing you, roll each breast up like a jelly roll to make a log and secure it with toothpicks. 4. Wrap 2 slices of bacon around each chicken breast log to cover the entire breast. Secure the bacon with toothpicks. 5. Place the chicken breast logs in the air fryer basket and air fry for 5 minutes, flip the logs over, and cook for another 5 minutes. Increase the heat to 390°F (199°C) and cook until the bacon is crisp, about 5 minutes more. 6. Remove the toothpicks and garnish with fresh rosemary sprigs, if desired, before serving. Store leftovers in an airtight container in the refrigerator for up to 4 days or in the freezer for up to a month. Reheat in a preheated 350°F (177°C) air fryer for 5 minutes, then increase the heat to 390°F (199°C) and cook for 2 minutes to crisp the bacon.

Tortilla Crusted Chicken Breast

Prep time: 10 minutes | Cook time: 12 minutes | Serves 2

⅓ cup flour	2 (3- to 4-ounce / 85- to 113-g)
1 teaspoon salt	boneless chicken breasts
1½ teaspoons chili powder	Vegetable oil
1 teaspoon ground cumin	½ cup salsa
Freshly ground black pepper, to	½ cup crumbled queso fresco
taste	Fresh cilantro leaves
1 egg, beaten	Sour cream or guacamole
¾ cup coarsely crushed yellow	(optional)
corn tortilla chips	

1. Set up a dredging station with three shallow dishes. Combine the flour, salt, chili powder, cumin and black pepper in the first shallow dish. Beat the egg in the second shallow dish. Place the crushed tortilla chips in the third shallow dish. 2. Dredge the chicken in the spiced flour, covering all sides of the breast. Then dip the chicken into the egg, coating the chicken completely. Finally, place the chicken into the tortilla chips and press the chips onto the chicken to make sure they adhere to all sides of the breast. Spray the coated chicken breasts on both sides with vegetable oil. 3. Preheat the air fryer to 380°F (193°C). 4. Air fry the chicken for 6 minutes. Then turn the chicken breasts over and air fry for another 6 minutes. (Increase the cooking time if you are using chicken breasts larger than 3 to 4 ounces / 85 to 113 g.) 5. When the chicken has finished cooking, serve each breast with a little salsa, the crumbled queso fresco and cilantro as the finishing touch. Serve some sour cream and/or guacamole at the table, if desired.

Cranberry Curry Chicken

Prep time: 12 minutes | Cook time: 18 minutes | Serves 4

3 (5-ounce / 142-g) low-sodium	½ cup low-sodium chicken
boneless, skinless chicken	broth
breasts, cut into 1½-inch cubes	⅓ cup dried cranberries
2 teaspoons olive oil	2 tablespoons freshly squeezed
2 tablespoons cornstarch	orange juice
1 tablespoon curry powder	Brown rice, cooked (optional)
1 tart apple, chopped	

Preheat the air fryer to 380°F (193°C). 2. In a medium bowl, mix the chicken and olive oil. Sprinkle with the cornstarch and curry powder. Toss to coat. Stir in the apple and transfer to a metal pan. Bake in the air fryer for 8 minutes, stirring once during cooking. 3. Add the chicken broth, cranberries, and orange juice. Bake for about 10 minutes more, or until the sauce is slightly thickened and the chicken reaches an internal temperature of 165°F (74°C) on a meat thermometer. Serve over hot cooked brown rice, if desired.

Crispy Dill Chicken Strips

Prep time: 30 minutes | Cook time: 10 minutes | Serves 4

2 whole boneless, skinless chicken breasts (about 1 pound / 454 g each), halved lengthwise	chips
	1 tablespoon dried dill weed
	1 tablespoon garlic powder
1 cup Italian dressing	1 large egg, beaten
3 cups finely crushed potato	1 to 2 tablespoons oil

1. In a large resealable bag, combine the chicken and Italian dressing. Seal the bag and refrigerate to marinate at least 1 hour. 2. In a shallow dish, stir together the potato chips, dill, and garlic powder. Place the beaten egg in a second shallow dish. 3. Remove the chicken from the marinade. Roll the chicken pieces in the egg and the potato chip mixture, coating thoroughly. 4. Preheat the air fryer to 325ºF (163ºC). Line the air fryer basket with parchment paper. 5. Place the coated chicken on the parchment and spritz with oil. 6. Cook for 5 minutes. Flip the chicken, spritz it with oil, and cook for 5 minutes more until the outsides are crispy and the insides are no longer pink.

Taco Chicken

Prep time: 10 minutes | Cook time: 23 minutes | Serves 4

2 large eggs	skinless chicken breasts or
1 tablespoon water	thighs, pounded to ¼ inch thick
Fine sea salt and ground black pepper, to taste	1 cup salsa
	1 cup shredded Monterey Jack
1 cup pork dust	cheese (about 4 ounces / 113 g)
1 teaspoon ground cumin	(omit for dairy-free)
1 teaspoon smoked paprika	Sprig of fresh cilantro, for
4 (5-ounce / 142-g) boneless,	garnish (optional)

1. Spray the air fryer basket with avocado oil. Preheat the air fryer to 400ºF (204ºC). 2. Crack the eggs into a shallow baking dish, add the water and a pinch each of salt and pepper, and whisk to combine. In another shallow baking dish, stir together the pork dust, cumin, and paprika until well combined. 3. Season the chicken breasts well on both sides with salt and pepper. Dip 1 chicken breast in the eggs and let any excess drip off, then dredge both sides of the chicken breast in the pork dust mixture. Spray the breast with avocado oil and place it in the air fryer basket. Repeat with the remaining 3 chicken breasts. 4. Air fry the chicken in the air fryer for 20 minutes, or until the internal temperature reaches 165ºF (74ºC) and the breading is golden brown, flipping halfway through. 5. Dollop each chicken breast with ¼ cup of the salsa and top with ¼ cup of the cheese. Return the breasts to the air fryer and cook for 3 minutes, or until the cheese is melted. Garnish with cilantro before serving, if desired. 6. Store leftovers in an airtight container in the refrigerator for up to 4 days. Reheat in a preheated 400ºF (204ºC) air fryer for 5 minutes, or until warmed through.

Chicken, Zucchini, and Spinach Salad

Prep time: 10 minutes | Cook time: 20 minutes | Serves 4

3 (5-ounce / 142-g) boneless, skinless chicken breasts, cut into 1-inch cubes	1 red bell pepper, sliced
	1 small zucchini, cut into strips
	3 tablespoons freshly squeezed
5 teaspoons extra-virgin olive oil	lemon juice
	6 cups fresh baby spinach
½ teaspoon dried thyme	leaves
1 medium red onion, sliced	

1. Insert the crisper plate into the basket and the basket into the unit. Preheat the unit by selecting AIR ROAST, setting the temperature to 375ºF (191ºC), and setting the time to 3 minutes. Select START/STOP to begin. 2. In a large bowl, combine the chicken, olive oil, and thyme. Toss to coat. Transfer to a medium metal bowl that fits into the basket. 3. Once the unit is preheated, place the bowl into the basket. 4. Select AIR ROAST, set the temperature to 375ºF (191ºC), and set the time to 20 minutes. Select START/STOP to begin. 5. After 8 minutes, add the red onion, red bell pepper, and zucchini to the bowl. Resume cooking. After about 6 minutes more, stir the chicken and vegetables. Resume cooking. 6. When the cooking is complete, a food thermometer inserted into the chicken should register at least 165ºF (74ºC). Remove the bowl from the unit and stir in the lemon juice. 7. Put the spinach in a serving bowl and top with the chicken mixture. Toss to combine and serve immediately.

Jerk Chicken Thighs

Prep time: 30 minutes | Cook time: 15 to 20 minutes | Serves 6

2 teaspoons ground coriander	½ teaspoon ground cinnamon
1 teaspoon ground allspice	½ teaspoon ground nutmeg
1 teaspoon cayenne pepper	2 pounds (907 g) boneless
1 teaspoon ground ginger	chicken thighs, skin on
1 teaspoon salt	2 tablespoons olive oil
1 teaspoon dried thyme	

1. In a small bowl, combine the coriander, allspice, cayenne, ginger, salt, thyme, cinnamon, and nutmeg. Stir until thoroughly combined. 2. Place the chicken in a baking dish and use paper towels to pat dry. Thoroughly coat both sides of the chicken with the spice mixture. Cover and refrigerate for at least 2 hours, preferably overnight. 3. Preheat the air fryer to 360ºF (182ºC). 4. Working in batches if necessary, arrange the chicken in a single layer in the air fryer basket and lightly coat with the olive oil. Pausing halfway through the cooking time to flip the chicken, air fry for 15 to 20 minutes, until a thermometer inserted into the thickest part registers 165ºF (74ºC).

Jalapeño Chicken Balls

Prep time: 10 minutes | Cook time: 25 minutes | Serves 4

1 medium red onion, minced	1 egg
2 garlic cloves, minced	1 teaspoon dried thyme
1 jalapeño pepper, minced	1 pound (454 g) ground chicken
2 teaspoons extra-virgin olive oil	breast
	Cooking oil spray
3 tablespoons ground almonds	

1. Insert the crisper plate into the basket and the basket into the unit. Preheat the unit by selecting BAKE, setting the temperature to 400°F (204°C), and setting the time to 3 minutes. Select START/STOP to begin. 2. In a 6-by-2-inch round pan, combine the red onion, garlic, jalapeño, and olive oil. 3. Once the unit is preheated, place the pan into the basket. 4. Select BAKE, set the temperature to 400°F (204°C), and set the time to 4 minutes. Select START/STOP to begin. 5. When the cooking is complete, the vegetables should be crisp-tender. Transfer to a medium bowl. 6. Mix the almonds, egg, and thyme into the vegetable mixture. Add the chicken and mix until just combined. Form the chicken mixture into about 24 (1-inch) balls. 7. Insert the crisper plate into the basket and the basket into the unit. Preheat the unit by selecting BAKE, setting the temperature to 400°F (204°C), and setting the time to 3 minutes. Select START/STOP to begin. 8. Once the unit is preheated, spray the crisper plate with cooking oil. Working in batches, place half the meatballs in a single layer, not touching, into the basket. 9. Select BAKE, set the temperature to 400°F (204°C), and set the time to 10 minutes. Select START/STOP to begin. 10. When the cooking is complete, a food thermometer inserted into the meatballs should register at least 165°F (74°C). 11. Repeat steps 8 and 9 with the remaining meatballs. Serve warm.

Personal Cauliflower Pizzas

Prep time: 10 minutes | Cook time: 25 minutes | Serves 2

1 (12-ounce / 340-g) bag frozen riced cauliflower	4 tablespoons no-sugar-added marinara sauce, divided
⅓ cup shredded Mozzarella cheese	4 ounces (113 g) fresh Mozzarella, chopped, divided
¼ cup almond flour	1 cup cooked chicken breast, chopped, divided
¼ grated Parmesan cheese	
1 large egg	½ cup chopped cherry tomatoes, divided
½ teaspoon salt	
1 teaspoon garlic powder	¼ cup fresh baby arugula, divided
1 teaspoon dried oregano	

1. Preheat the air fryer to 400°F (204°C). Cut 4 sheets of parchment paper to fit the basket of the air fryer. Brush with olive oil and set aside. 2. In a large glass bowl, microwave the cauliflower according to package directions. Place the cauliflower on a clean towel, draw up the sides, and squeeze tightly over a sink to remove the excess moisture. Return the cauliflower to the bowl and add the shredded Mozzarella along with the almond flour, Parmesan, egg, salt, garlic powder, and oregano. Stir until thoroughly combined. 3. Divide the dough into two equal portions. Place one piece of dough on the prepared parchment paper and pat gently into a thin, flat disk 7 to 8 inches in diameter. Air fry for 15 minutes until the crust begins to brown. Let cool for 5 minutes. 4. Transfer the parchment paper with the crust on top to a baking sheet. Place a second sheet of parchment paper over the crust. While holding the edges of both sheets together, carefully lift the crust off the baking sheet, flip it, and place it back in the air fryer basket. The new sheet of parchment paper is now on the bottom. Remove the top piece of paper and air fry the crust for another 15 minutes until the top begins to brown. Remove the basket from the air fryer. 5. Spread 2 tablespoons of the marinara sauce on top of the crust, followed by half the fresh Mozzarella, chicken, cherry tomatoes, and arugula. Air fry for 5 to 10 minutes longer, until the cheese is melted and beginning to brown. Remove the pizza from the oven and let it sit for 10 minutes before serving. Repeat with the remaining ingredients to make a second pizza.

African Piri-Piri Chicken Drumsticks

Prep time: 30 minutes | Cook time: 20 minutes | Serves 2

Chicken:	1 teaspoon smoked paprika
1 tablespoon chopped fresh thyme leaves	½ teaspoon kosher salt
	½ teaspoon black pepper
1 tablespoon minced fresh ginger	4 chicken drumsticks
	Glaze:
1 small shallot, finely chopped	2 tablespoons butter or ghee
2 garlic cloves, minced	1 teaspoon chopped fresh thyme leaves
⅓ cup piri-piri sauce or hot sauce	
	1 garlic clove, minced
3 tablespoons extra-virgin olive oil	1 tablespoon piri-piri sauce
	1 tablespoon fresh lemon juice
Zest and juice of 1 lemon	

1. For the chicken: In a small bowl, stir together all the ingredients except the chicken. Place the chicken and the marinade in a gallon-size resealable plastic bag. Seal the bag and massage to coat. Refrigerate for at least 2 hours or up to 24 hours, turning the bag occasionally. 2. Place the chicken legs in the air fryer basket. Set the air fryer to 400°F (204°C) for 20 minutes, turning the chicken halfway through the cooking time. 3. Meanwhile, for the glaze: Melt the butter in a small saucepan over medium-high heat. Add the thyme and garlic. Cook, stirring, until the garlic just begins to brown, 1 to 2 minutes. Add the piri-piri sauce and lemon juice. Reduce the heat to medium-low and simmer for 1 to 2 minutes. 4. Transfer the chicken to a serving platter. Pour the glaze over the chicken. Serve immediately.

Classic Whole Chicken

Prep time: 5 minutes | Cook time: 50 minutes | Serves 4

Oil, for spraying
1 (4-pound / 1.8-kg) whole chicken, giblets removed
1 tablespoon olive oil
1 teaspoon paprika
½ teaspoon granulated garlic

½ teaspoon salt
½ teaspoon freshly ground black pepper
¼ teaspoon finely chopped fresh parsley, for garnish

1. Line the air fryer basket with parchment and spray lightly with oil. 2. Pat the chicken dry with paper towels. Rub it with the olive oil until evenly coated. 3. In a small bowl, mix together the paprika, garlic, salt, and black pepper and sprinkle it evenly over the chicken. 4. Place the chicken in the prepared basket, breast-side down. 5. Air fry at 360ºF (182ºC) for 30 minutes, flip, and cook for another 20 minutes, or until the internal temperature reaches 165ºF (74ºC) and the juices run clear. 6. Sprinkle with the parsley before serving.

Chicken Wellington

Prep time: 30 minutes | Cook time: 31 minutes | Serves 2

2 (5-ounce / 142-g) boneless, skinless chicken breasts
½ cup White Worcestershire sauce
3 tablespoons butter
½ cup finely diced onion (about ½ onion)
8 ounces (227 g) button mushrooms, finely chopped
¼ cup chicken stock

2 tablespoons White Worcestershire sauce (or white wine)
Salt and freshly ground black pepper, to taste
1 tablespoon chopped fresh tarragon
2 sheets puff pastry, thawed
1 egg, beaten
Vegetable oil

1. Place the chicken breasts in a shallow dish. Pour the White Worcestershire sauce over the chicken coating both sides and marinate for 30 minutes. 2. While the chicken is marinating, melt the butter in a large skillet over medium-high heat on the stovetop. Add the onion and sauté for a few minutes, until it starts to soften. Add the mushrooms and sauté for 3 to 5 minutes until the vegetables are brown and soft. Deglaze the skillet with the chicken stock, scraping up any bits from the bottom of the pan. Add the White Worcestershire sauce and simmer for 2 to 3 minutes until the mixture reduces and starts to thicken. Season with salt and freshly ground black pepper. Remove the mushroom mixture from the heat and stir in the fresh tarragon. Let the mushroom mixture cool. 3. Preheat the air fryer to 360ºF (182ºC). 4. Remove the chicken from the marinade and transfer it to the air fryer basket. Tuck the small end of the chicken breast under the thicker part to shape it into a circle rather than an oval. Pour the marinade over the chicken and air fry for 10 minutes. 5. Roll out the puff pastry and cut out two 6-inch squares. Brush the perimeter of each square with the egg wash. Place half of the mushroom mixture in the center of each puff pastry square. Place the chicken breasts, top side down on the mushroom mixture. Starting with one corner of puff pastry and working in one direction, pull the pastry up over the chicken to enclose it and press the ends of the pastry together in the middle. Brush the pastry with the egg wash to seal the edges. Turn the Wellingtons over and set aside. 6. Make a decorative design with the remaining puff pastry, cut out four 10-inch strips. For each Wellington, twist two of the strips together, place them over the chicken breast wrapped in puff pastry, and tuck the ends underneath to seal it. Brush the entire top and sides of the Wellingtons with the egg wash. 7. Preheat the air fryer to 350ºF (177ºC). 8. Spray or brush the air fryer basket with vegetable oil. Air fry the chicken Wellingtons for 13 minutes. Carefully turn the Wellingtons over. Air fry for another 8 minutes. Transfer to serving plates, light a candle and enjoy!

Lemon-Basil Turkey Breasts

Prep time: 30 minutes | Cook time: 58 minutes | Serves 4

2 tablespoons olive oil
2 pounds (907 g) turkey breasts, bone-in, skin-on
Coarse sea salt and ground black pepper, to taste

1 teaspoon fresh basil leaves, chopped
2 tablespoons lemon zest, grated

1. Rub olive oil on all sides of the turkey breasts; sprinkle with salt, pepper, basil, and lemon zest. 2. Place the turkey breasts skin side up on the parchment-lined air fryer basket. 3. Cook in the preheated air fryer at 330ºF (166ºC) for 30 minutes. Now, turn them over and cook an additional 28 minutes. 4. Serve with lemon wedges, if desired. Bon appétit!

Cilantro Lime Chicken Thighs

Prep time: 15 minutes | Cook time: 22 minutes | Serves 4

4 bone-in, skin-on chicken thighs
1 teaspoon baking powder
½ teaspoon garlic powder

2 teaspoons chili powder
1 teaspoon cumin
2 medium limes
¼ cup chopped fresh cilantro

1. Pat chicken thighs dry and sprinkle with baking powder. 2. In a small bowl, mix garlic powder, chili powder, and cumin and sprinkle evenly over thighs, gently rubbing on and under chicken skin. 3. Cut one lime in half and squeeze juice over thighs. Place chicken into the air fryer basket. 4. Adjust the temperature to 380ºF (193ºC) and roast for 22 minutes. 5. Cut other lime into four wedges for serving and garnish cooked chicken with wedges and cilantro.

General Tso's Chicken

Prep time: 10 minutes | Cook time: 14 minutes | Serves 4

1 tablespoon sesame oil
1 teaspoon minced garlic
½ teaspoon ground ginger
1 cup chicken broth
4 tablespoons soy sauce, divided
½ teaspoon sriracha, plus more for serving
2 tablespoons hoisin sauce

4 tablespoons cornstarch, divided
4 boneless, skinless chicken breasts, cut into 1-inch pieces
Olive oil spray
2 medium scallions, sliced, green parts only
Sesame seeds, for garnish

1. In a small saucepan over low heat, combine the sesame oil, garlic, and ginger and cook for 1 minute. 2. Add the chicken broth, 2 tablespoons of soy sauce, the sriracha, and hoisin. Whisk to combine. 3. Whisk in 2 tablespoons of cornstarch and continue cooking over low heat until the sauce starts to thicken, about 5 minutes. Remove the pan from the heat, cover it, and set aside. 4. Insert the crisper plate into the basket and the basket into the unit. Preheat the unit by selecting BAKE, setting the temperature to 400ºF (204ºC), and setting the time to 3 minutes. Select START/STOP to begin. 5. In a medium bowl, toss together the chicken, remaining 2 tablespoons of soy sauce, and remaining 2 tablespoons of cornstarch. 6. Once the unit is preheated, spray the crisper plate with olive oil. Place the chicken into the basket and spray it with olive oil. 7. Select BAKE, set the temperature to 400ºF (204ºC), and set the time to 9 minutes. Select START/STOP to begin. 8. After 5 minutes, remove the basket, shake, and spray the chicken with more olive oil. Reinsert the basket to resume cooking. 9. When the cooking is complete, a food thermometer inserted into the chicken should register at least 165ºF (74ºC). Transfer the chicken to a large bowl and toss it with the sauce. Garnish with the scallions and sesame seeds and serve.

French Garlic Chicken

Prep time: 30 minutes | Cook time: 27 minutes | Serves 4

2 tablespoon extra-virgin olive oil
1 tablespoon Dijon mustard
1 tablespoon apple cider vinegar
3 cloves garlic, minced
2 teaspoons herbes de Provence
½ teaspoon kosher salt

1 teaspoon black pepper
1 pound (454 g) boneless, skinless chicken thighs, halved crosswise
2 tablespoons butter
8 cloves garlic, chopped
¼ cup heavy whipping cream

1. In a small bowl, combine the olive oil, mustard, vinegar, minced garlic, herbes de Provence, salt, and pepper. Use a wire whisk to emulsify the mixture. 2. Pierce the chicken all over with a fork to allow the marinade to penetrate better. Place the chicken in a resealable plastic bag, pour the marinade over, and seal. Massage

until the chicken is well coated. Marinate at room temperature for 30 minutes or in the refrigerator for up to 24 hours. 3. When you are ready to cook, place the butter and chopped garlic in a baking pan and place it in the air fryer basket. Set the air fryer to 400ºF (204ºC) for 5 minutes, or until the butter has melted and the garlic is sizzling. 4. Add the chicken and the marinade to the seasoned butter. Set the air fryer to 350ºF (177ºC) for 15 minutes. Use a meat thermometer to ensure the chicken has reached an internal temperature of 165ºF (74ºC). Transfer the chicken to a plate and cover lightly with foil to keep warm. 5. Add the cream to the pan, stirring to combine with the garlic, butter, and cooking juices. Place the pan in the air fryer basket. Set the air fryer to 350ºF (177ºC) for 7 minutes. 6. Pour the thickened sauce over the chicken and serve.

Thai-Style Cornish Game Hens

Prep time: 30 minutes | Cook time: 20 minutes | Serves 4

1 cup chopped fresh cilantro leaves and stems
¼ cup fish sauce
1 tablespoon soy sauce
1 serrano chile, seeded and chopped
8 garlic cloves, smashed
2 tablespoons sugar

2 tablespoons lemongrass paste
2 teaspoons black pepper
2 teaspoons ground coriander
1 teaspoon kosher salt
1 teaspoon ground turmeric
2 Cornish game hens, giblets removed, split in half lengthwise

1. In a blender, combine the cilantro, fish sauce, soy sauce, serrano, garlic, sugar, lemongrass, black pepper, coriander, salt, and turmeric. Blend until smooth. 2. Place the game hen halves in a large bowl. Pour the cilantro mixture over the hen halves and toss to coat. Marinate at room temperature for 30 minutes, or cover and refrigerate for up to 24 hours. 3. Arrange the hen halves in a single layer in the air fryer basket. Set the air fryer to 400ºF (204ºC) for 20 minutes. Use a meat thermometer to ensure the game hens have reached an internal temperature of 165ºF (74ºC).

Chicken Legs with Leeks

Prep time: 30 minutes | Cook time: 18 minutes | Serves 6

2 leeks, sliced
2 large-sized tomatoes, chopped
3 cloves garlic, minced
½ teaspoon dried oregano
6 chicken legs, boneless and

skinless
½ teaspoon smoked cayenne pepper
2 tablespoons olive oil
A freshly ground nutmeg

1. In a mixing dish, thoroughly combine all ingredients, minus the leeks. Place in the refrigerator and let it marinate overnight. 2. Lay the leeks onto the bottom of the air fryer basket. Top with the chicken legs. 3. Roast chicken legs at 375ºF (191ºC) for 18 minutes, turning halfway through. Serve with hoisin sauce.

Chipotle Aioli Wings

Prep time: 5 minutes | Cook time: 25 minutes | Serves 6

2 pounds (907 g) bone-in chicken wings	pepper
½ teaspoon salt	2 tablespoons mayonnaise
¼ teaspoon ground black	2 teaspoons chipotle powder
	2 tablespoons lemon juice

1. In a large bowl, toss wings in salt and pepper, then place into ungreased air fryer basket. Adjust the temperature to 400ºF (204ºC) and air fry for 25 minutes, shaking the basket twice while cooking. Wings will be done when golden and have an internal temperature of at least 165ºF (74ºC). 2. In a small bowl, whisk together mayonnaise, chipotle powder, and lemon juice. Place cooked wings into a large serving bowl and drizzle with aioli. Toss to coat. Serve warm.

Fajita Chicken Strips

Prep time: 10 minutes | Cook time: 15 minutes | Serves 4

1 pound (454 g) boneless, skinless chicken tenderloins, cut into strips	1 onion, cut into chunks
	1 tablespoon olive oil
3 bell peppers, any color, cut into chunks	1 tablespoon fajita seasoning mix
	Cooking spray

Preheat the air fryer to 370ºF (188ºC). 2. In a large bowl, mix together the chicken, bell peppers, onion, olive oil, and fajita seasoning mix until completely coated. 3. Spray the air fryer basket lightly with cooking spray. 4. Place the chicken and vegetables in the air fryer basket and lightly spray with cooking spray. 5. Air fry for 7 minutes. Shake the basket and air fry for an additional 5 to 8 minutes, until the chicken is cooked through and the veggies are starting to char. 6. Serve warm.

Stuffed Chicken Florentine

Prep time: 10 minutes | Cook time: 20 minutes | Serves 4

3 tablespoons pine nuts	Salt and freshly ground black pepper, to taste
¾ cup frozen spinach, thawed and squeezed dry	
	4 small boneless, skinless chicken breast halves (about 1½ pounds / 680 g)
⅓ cup ricotta cheese	
2 tablespoons grated Parmesan cheese	
3 cloves garlic, minced	8 slices bacon

1. Place the pine nuts in a small pan and set in the air fryer basket. Set the air fryer to 400ºF (204ºC) and air fry for 2 to 3 minutes until toasted. Remove the pine nuts to a mixing bowl and continue preheating the air fryer. 2. In a large bowl, combine the spinach, ricotta, Parmesan, and garlic. Season to taste with salt and pepper and stir well until thoroughly combined. 3. Using a sharp knife, cut into the chicken breasts, slicing them across and opening them up like a book, but be careful not to cut them all the way through. Sprinkle the chicken with salt and pepper. 4. Spoon equal amounts of the spinach mixture into the chicken, then fold the top of the chicken breast back over the top of the stuffing. Wrap each chicken breast with 2 slices of bacon. 5. Working in batches if necessary, air fry the chicken for 18 to 20 minutes until the bacon is crisp and a thermometer inserted into the thickest part of the chicken registers 165ºF (74ºC).

Chicken Drumsticks with Barbecue-Honey Sauce

Prep time: 5 minutes | Cook time: 40 minutes | Serves 5

1 tablespoon olive oil	Salt and ground black pepper, to taste
10 chicken drumsticks	
Chicken seasoning or rub, to taste	1 cup barbecue sauce
	¼ cup honey

1. Preheat the air fryer to 390ºF (199ºC). Grease the air fryer basket with olive oil. 2. Rub the chicken drumsticks with chicken seasoning or rub, salt and ground black pepper on a clean work surface. 3. Arrange the chicken drumsticks in a single layer in the air fryer, then air fry for 18 minutes or until lightly browned. Flip the drumsticks halfway through. You may need to work in batches to avoid overcrowding. 4. Meanwhile, combine the barbecue sauce and honey in a small bowl. Stir to mix well. 5. Remove the drumsticks from the air fryer and baste with the sauce mixture to serve.

Cheese-Encrusted Chicken Tenderloins with Peanuts

Prep time: 10 minutes | Cook time: 25 minutes | Serves 4

½ cup grated Parmesan cheese	1½ pounds (680 g) chicken tenderloins
½ teaspoon garlic powder	
1 teaspoon red pepper flakes	2 tablespoons peanuts, roasted and roughly chopped
Sea salt and ground black pepper, to taste	
	Cooking spray
2 tablespoons peanut oil	

Preheat the air fryer to 360ºF (182ºC). Spritz the air fryer basket with cooking spray. 2. Combine the Parmesan cheese, garlic powder, red pepper flakes, salt, black pepper, and peanut oil in a large bow. Stir to mix well. 3. Dip the chicken tenderloins in the cheese mixture, then press to coat well. Shake the excess off. 4. Transfer the chicken tenderloins in the air fryer basket. Air fry for 12 minutes or until well browned. Flip the tenderloin halfway through. You may need to work in batches to avoid overcrowding. 5. Transfer the chicken tenderloins on a large plate and top with roasted peanuts before serving.

Chapter 3 Beef, Pork, and Lamb

Blue Cheese Steak Salad

Prep time: 30 minutes | Cook time: 22 minutes | Serves 4

2 tablespoons balsamic vinegar
2 tablespoons red wine vinegar
1 tablespoon Dijon mustard
1 tablespoon Swerve
1 teaspoon minced garlic
Sea salt and freshly ground
black pepper, to taste
¾ cup extra-virgin olive oil
1 pound (454 g) boneless sirloin
steak
Avocado oil spray
1 small red onion, cut into
¼-inch-thick rounds
6 ounces (170 g) lettuce
½ cup cherry tomatoes, halved
3 ounces (85 g) blue cheese,
crumbled

1. In a blender, combine the balsamic vinegar, red wine vinegar, Dijon mustard, Swerve, and garlic. Season with salt and pepper and process until smooth. With the blender running, drizzle in the olive oil. Process until well combined. Transfer to a jar with a tight-fitting lid, and refrigerate until ready to serve (it will keep for up to 2 weeks). 2. Season the steak with salt and pepper and let sit at room temperature for at least 45 minutes, time permitting. 3. Set the air fryer to 400°F (204°C). Spray the steak with oil and place it in the air fryer basket. Air fry for 6 minutes. Flip the steak and spray it with more oil. Air fry for 6 minutes more for medium-rare or until the steak is done to your liking. 4. Transfer the steak to a plate, tent with a piece of aluminum foil, and allow it to rest. 5. Spray the onion slices with oil and place them in the air fryer basket. Cook at 400°F (204°C) for 5 minutes. Flip the onion slices and spray them with more oil. Air fry for 5 minutes more. 6. Slice the steak diagonally into thin strips. Place the lettuce, cherry tomatoes, onion slices, and steak in a large bowl. Toss with the desired amount of dressing. Sprinkle with crumbled blue cheese and serve.

Greek-Style Meatloaf

Prep time: 5 minutes | Cook time: 25 minutes | Serves 6

1 pound (454 g) lean ground
beef
2 eggs
2 Roma tomatoes, diced
½ white onion, diced
½ cup whole wheat bread
crumbs
1 teaspoon garlic powder
1 teaspoon dried oregano
1 teaspoon dried thyme
1 teaspoon salt
1 teaspoon black pepper
2 ounces (57 g) mozzarella
cheese, shredded
1 tablespoon olive oil
Fresh chopped parsley, for
garnish

1. Preheat the oven to 380°F(193°C). 2. In a large bowl, mix together the ground beef, eggs, tomatoes, onion, bread crumbs, garlic powder, oregano, thyme, salt, pepper, and cheese. 3. Form into a loaf, flattening to 1-inch thick. 4. Brush the top with olive oil, then place the meatloaf into the air fryer basket and cook for 25 minutes. 5. Remove from the air fryer and allow to rest for 5 minutes, before slicing and serving with a sprinkle of parsley.

Pork Schnitzel with Dill Sauce

Prep time: 5 minutes | Cook time: 24 minutes | Serves 4 to 6

6 boneless, center cut pork chops (about 1½ pounds / 680 g)
½ cup flour
1½ teaspoons salt
Freshly ground black pepper, to taste
2 eggs
½ cup milk
1½ cups toasted fine bread crumbs
1 teaspoon paprika

3 tablespoons butter, melted
2 tablespoons vegetable or olive oil
lemon wedges
Dill Sauce:
1 cup chicken stock
1½ tablespoons cornstarch
⅓ cup sour cream
1½ tablespoons chopped fresh dill
Salt and pepper, to taste

1. Trim the excess fat from the pork chops and pound each chop with a meat mallet between two pieces of plastic wrap until they are ½-inch thick. 2. Set up a dredging station. Combine the flour, salt, and black pepper in a shallow dish. Whisk the eggs and milk together in a second shallow dish. Finally, combine the bread crumbs and paprika in a third shallow dish. 3. Dip each flattened pork chop in the flour. Shake off the excess flour and dip each chop into the egg mixture. Finally dip them into the bread crumbs and press the bread crumbs onto the meat firmly. Place each finished chop on a baking sheet until they are all coated. 4. Preheat the air fryer to 400ºF (204ºC). 5. Combine the melted butter and the oil in a small bowl and lightly brush both sides of the coated pork chops. Do not brush the chops too heavily or the breading will not be as crispy. 6. Air fry one schnitzel at a time for 4 minutes, turning it over halfway through the cooking time. Hold the cooked schnitzels warm on a baking pan in a 170ºF (77ºC) oven while you finish air frying the rest. 7. While the schnitzels are cooking, whisk the chicken stock and cornstarch together in a small saucepan over medium-high heat on the stovetop. Bring the mixture to a boil and simmer for 2 minutes. Remove the saucepan from heat and whisk in the sour cream. Add the chopped fresh dill and season with salt and pepper. 8. Transfer the pork schnitzel to a platter and serve with dill sauce and lemon wedges.

Kheema Burgers

Prep time: 15 minutes | Cook time: 12 minutes | Serves 4

Burgers:
1 pound (454 g) 85% lean ground beef or ground lamb
2 large eggs, lightly beaten
1 medium yellow onion, diced
¼ cup chopped fresh cilantro
1 tablespoon minced fresh ginger
3 cloves garlic, minced
2 teaspoons garam masala
1 teaspoon ground turmeric
½ teaspoon ground cinnamon

⅛ teaspoon ground cardamom
1 teaspoon kosher salt
1 teaspoon cayenne pepper
Raita Sauce:
1 cup grated cucumber
½ cup sour cream
¼ teaspoon kosher salt
¼ teaspoon black pepper
For Serving:
4 lettuce leaves, hamburger buns, or naan breads

1. For the burgers: In a large bowl, combine the ground beef, eggs, onion, cilantro, ginger, garlic, garam masala, turmeric, cinnamon, cardamom, salt, and cayenne. Gently mix until ingredients are thoroughly combined. 2. Divide the meat into four portions and form into round patties. Make a slight depression in the middle of each patty with your thumb to prevent them from puffing up into a dome shape while cooking. 3. Place the patties in the air fryer basket. Set the air fryer to 350ºF (177ºC) for 12 minutes. Use a meat thermometer to ensure the burgers have reached an internal temperature of 160ºF / 71ºC (for medium). 4. Meanwhile, for the sauce: In a small bowl, combine the cucumber, sour cream, salt, and pepper. 5. To serve: Place the burgers on the lettuce, buns, or naan and top with the sauce.

Beef Empanadas

Prep time: 15 minutes | Cook time: 25 minutes | Serves 5

2 garlic cloves, chopped
⅓ cup chopped green bell
pepper
⅓ medium onion, chopped
8 ounces (227 g) 93% lean
ground beef
1 teaspoon hamburger
seasoning
Salt and freshly ground black

pepper, to taste
15 empanada wrappers
1 cup shredded Mozzarella
cheese
1 cup shredded pepper Jack
cheese
1 tablespoon butter
Cooking oil spray

1. Spray a skillet with the cooking oil and place it over medium-high heat. Add the garlic, green bell pepper, and onion. Cook until fragrant, about 2 minutes. 2. Add the ground beef to the skillet. Season it with the hamburger seasoning, salt, and pepper. Using a spatula or spoon, break up the beef into small pieces. Cook the beef for about 5 minutes until browned. Drain any excess fat. 3. Lay the empanada wrappers on a work surface. 4. Dip a basting brush in water. Glaze each wrapper along the edges with the wet brush. This will soften the crust and make it easier to roll. You can also dip your fingers in water to moisten the edges. 5. Scoop 2 to 3 tablespoons of the ground beef mixture onto each empanada wrapper. Sprinkle the Mozzarella and pepper Jack cheeses over the beef. 6. Close the empanadas by folding the empanada wrapper in half over the filling. Using the back of a fork, press along the edges to seal. 7. Insert the crisper plate into the basket and the basket into the unit. Preheat the unit by selecting AIR FRY, setting the temperature to 400°F (204°C), and setting the time to 3 minutes. Select START/STOP to begin. 8. Once the unit is preheated, spray the crisper plate with cooking oil. Working in batches, place 7 or 8 empanadas into the basket. Spray each with cooking oil. 9. Select AIR FRY, set the temperature to 400°F (204°C), and set the time to 12 minutes. Select START/STOP to begin. 10. After 8 minutes, flip the empanadas and spray them with more cooking oil. Resume cooking. 11. When the cooking is complete, transfer the empanadas to a plate. For added flavor, top each hot empanada with a bit of butter and let melt. Repeat steps 8, 9, and 10 for the remaining empanadas. 12. Cool for 5 minutes before serving.

Spinach and Provolone Steak Rolls

Prep time: 10 minutes | Cook time: 12 minutes |
Makes 8 rolls

1 (1-pound / 454-g) flank steak,
butterflied
8 (1-ounce / 28-g, ¼-inch-thick)
deli slices provolone cheese

1 cup fresh spinach leaves
½ teaspoon salt
¼ teaspoon ground black
pepper

1. Place steak on a large plate. Place provolone slices to cover steak, leaving 1-inch at the edges. Lay spinach leaves over cheese. Gently roll steak and tie with kitchen twine or secure with toothpicks. Carefully slice into eight pieces. Sprinkle each with salt and pepper. 2. Place rolls into ungreased air fryer basket, cut side up. Adjust the temperature to 400°F (204°C) and air fry for 12 minutes. Steak rolls will be browned and cheese will be melted when done and have an internal temperature of at least 150°F (66°C) for medium steak and 180°F (82°C) for well-done steak. Serve warm.

Beef Chuck Cheeseburgers

Prep time: 10 minutes | Cook time: 15 minutes | Serves 4

¾ pound (340 g) ground beef chuck

1 envelope onion soup mix

Kosher salt and freshly ground black pepper, to taste

1 teaspoon paprika

4 slices Monterey Jack cheese

4 ciabatta rolls

For serve:

Letture

Tomato

1. In a bowl, stir together the ground chuck, onion soup mix, salt, black pepper, and paprika to combine well. 2. Preheat the air fryer to 385ºF (196ºC). 3. Take four equal portions of the mixture and mold each one into a patty. Transfer to the air fryer and air fry for 10 minutes. 4. Put the slices of cheese, letture, and tomato on the top of the burgers. 5. Air fry for another minute before serving on ciabatta rolls.

Korean Beef Tacos

Prep time: 30 minutes | Cook time: 12 minutes | Serves 6

2 tablespoons gochujang (Korean red chile paste)

2 cloves garlic, minced

2 teaspoons minced fresh ginger

2 tablespoons toasted sesame oil

1 tablespoon soy sauce

2 tablespoons sesame seeds

2 teaspoons sugar

½ teaspoon kosher salt

1½ pounds (680 g) thinly sliced beef (chuck, rib eye, or sirloin)

1 medium red onion, sliced

12 (6-inch) flour tortillas, warmed; or lettuce leaves

½ cup chopped green onions

¼ cup chopped fresh cilantro (optional)

½ cup kimchi (optional)

1. In a small bowl, combine the gochujang, garlic, ginger, sesame oil, soy sauce, sesame seeds, sugar, and salt. Whisk until well combined. Place the beef and red onion in a resealable plastic bag and pour the marinade over. Seal the bag and massage to coat all of the meat and onion. Marinate at room temperature for 30 minutes or in the refrigerator for up to 24 hours. 2. Place the meat and onion in the air fryer basket, leaving behind as much of the marinade as possible; discard the marinade. Set the air fryer to 400ºF (204ºC) for 12 minutes, shaking halfway through the cooking time. 3. To serve, place meat and onion in the tortillas. Top with the green onions and the cilantro and kimchi, if using, and serve.

Beef and Goat Cheese Stuffed Peppers

Prep time: 10 minutes | Cook time: 30 minutes | Serves 4

1 pound (454 g) lean ground beef

½ cup cooked brown rice

2 Roma tomatoes, diced

3 garlic cloves, minced

½ yellow onion, diced

2 tablespoons fresh oregano, chopped

1 teaspoon salt

½ teaspoon black pepper

¼ teaspoon ground allspice

2 bell peppers, halved and seeded

4 ounces (113 g) goat cheese

¼ cup fresh parsley, chopped

1. Preheat the air fryer to 360°F(182°C). 2. In a large bowl, combine the ground beef, rice, tomatoes, garlic, onion, oregano, salt, pepper, and allspice. Mix well. 3. Divide the beef mixture equally into the halved bell peppers and top each with about 1 ounce (28 g a quarter of the total) of the goat cheese. 4. Place the peppers into the air fryer basket in a single layer, making sure that they don't touch each other. Bake for 30 minutes. 5. Remove the peppers from the air fryer and top with fresh parsley before serving.

Beef Loin with Thyme and Parsley

Prep time: 5 minutes | Cook time: 15 minutes | Serves 4

1 tablespoon butter, melted

¼ dried thyme

1 teaspoon garlic salt

¼ teaspoon dried parsley

1 pound (454 g) beef loin

1. Preheat the air fryer to 400ºF (204ºC). 2. In a bowl, combine the melted butter, thyme, garlic salt, and parsley. 3. Cut the beef loin into slices and generously apply the seasoned butter using a brush. Transfer to the air fryer basket. 4. Air fry the beef for 15 minutes. 5. Take care when removing it and serve hot.

Beef and Pork Sausage Meatloaf

Prep time: 20 minutes | Cook time: 25 minutes | Serves 4

¾ pound (340 g) ground chuck
4 ounces (113 g) ground pork
sausage
1 cup shallots, finely chopped
2 eggs, well beaten
3 tablespoons plain milk
1 tablespoon oyster sauce
1 teaspoon porcini mushrooms

½ teaspoon cumin powder
1 teaspoon garlic paste
1 tablespoon fresh parsley
Salt and crushed red pepper
flakes, to taste
1 cup crushed saltines
Cooking spray

1. Preheat the air fryer to 360ºF (182ºC). Spritz a baking dish with cooking spray. 2. Mix all the ingredients in a large bowl, combining everything well. 3. Transfer to the baking dish and bake in the air fryer for 25 minutes. 4. Serve hot.

Bulgogi Burgers

Prep time: 30 minutes | Cook time: 10 minutes | Serves 4

Burgers:
1 pound (454 g) 85% lean
ground beef
¼ cup chopped scallions
2 tablespoons gochujang
(Korean red chile paste)
1 tablespoon dark soy sauce
2 teaspoons minced garlic
2 teaspoons minced fresh ginger
2 teaspoons sugar

1 tablespoon toasted sesame oil
½ teaspoon kosher salt
Gochujang Mayonnaise:
¼ cup mayonnaise
¼ cup chopped scallions
1 tablespoon gochujang (Korean
red chile paste)
1 tablespoon toasted sesame oil
2 teaspoons sesame seeds
4 hamburger buns

1. For the burgers: In a large bowl, mix the ground beef, scallions, gochujang, soy sauce, garlic, ginger, sugar, sesame oil, and salt. Marinate at room temperature for 30 minutes, or cover and refrigerate for up to 24 hours. 2. Divide the meat into four portions and form them into round patties. Make a slight depression in the middle of each patty with your thumb to prevent them from puffing up into a dome shape while cooking. 3. Place the patties in a single layer in the air fryer basket. Set the air fryer to 350ºF (177ºC) for 10 minutes. 4. Meanwhile, for the gochujang mayonnaise: Stir together the mayonnaise, scallions, gochujang, sesame oil, and sesame seeds. 5. At the end of the cooking time, use a meat thermometer to ensure the burgers have reached an internal temperature of 160ºF / 71ºC (medium). 6. To serve, place the burgers on the buns and top with the mayonnaise.

Pork Meatballs

Prep time: 10 minutes | Cook time: 12 minutes | Makes 18 meatballs

1 pound (454 g) ground pork
1 large egg, whisked
½ teaspoon garlic powder
½ teaspoon salt
½ teaspoon ground ginger
¼ teaspoon crushed red pepper flakes
1 medium scallion, trimmed and sliced

1. Combine all ingredients in a large bowl. Spoon out 2 tablespoons mixture and roll into a ball. Repeat to form eighteen meatballs total. 2. Place meatballs into ungreased air fryer basket. Adjust the temperature to 400ºF (204ºC) and air fry for 12 minutes, shaking the basket three times throughout cooking. Meatballs will be browned and have an internal temperature of at least 145ºF (63ºC) when done. Serve warm.

Spicy Lamb Sirloin Chops

Prep time: 30 minutes | Cook time: 15 minutes | Serves 4

½ yellow onion, coarsely chopped
4 coin-size slices peeled fresh ginger
5 garlic cloves
1 teaspoon garam masala
1 teaspoon ground fennel
1 teaspoon ground cinnamon
1 teaspoon ground turmeric
½ to 1 teaspoon cayenne pepper
½ teaspoon ground cardamom
1 teaspoon kosher salt
1 pound (454 g) lamb sirloin chops

1. In a blender, combine the onion, ginger, garlic, garam masala, fennel, cinnamon, turmeric, cayenne, cardamom, and salt. Pulse until the onion is finely minced and the mixture forms a thick paste, 3 to 4 minutes. 2. Place the lamb chops in a large bowl. Slash the meat and fat with a sharp knife several times to allow the marinade to penetrate better. Add the spice paste to the bowl and toss the lamb to coat. Marinate at room temperature for 30 minutes or cover and refrigerate for up to 24 hours. 3. Place the lamb chops in a single layer in the air fryer basket. Set the air fryer to 325ºF (163ºC) for 15 minutes, turning the chops halfway through the cooking time. Use a meat thermometer to ensure the lamb has reached an internal temperature of 145ºF (63ºC) (medium-rare).

Deconstructed Chicago Dogs

Prep time: 10 minutes | Cook time: 7 minutes | Serves 4

4 hot dogs

2 large dill pickles

¼ cup diced onions

1 tomato, cut into ½-inch dice

4 pickled sport peppers, diced

For Garnish (Optional):

Brown mustard

Celery salt

Poppy seeds

1. Spray the air fryer basket with avocado oil. Preheat the air fryer to 400ºF (204ºC). 2. Place the hot dogs in the air fryer basket and air fry for 5 to 7 minutes, until hot and slightly crispy. 3. While the hot dogs cook, quarter one of the dill pickles lengthwise, so that you have 4 pickle spears. Finely dice the other pickle. 4. When the hot dogs are done, transfer them to a serving platter and arrange them in a row, alternating with the pickle spears. Top with the diced pickles, onions, tomato, and sport peppers. Drizzle brown mustard on top and garnish with celery salt and poppy seeds, if desired. 5. Best served fresh. Store leftover hot dogs in an airtight container in the refrigerator for up to 3 days. Reheat in a preheated 390ºF (199ºC) air fryer for 2 minutes, or until warmed through.

Provolone Stuffed Beef and Pork Meatballs

Prep time: 15 minutes | Cook time: 12 minutes | Serves 4 to 6

1 tablespoon olive oil

1 small onion, finely chopped

1 to 2 cloves garlic, minced

¾ pound (340 g) ground beef

¾ pound (340 g) ground pork

¾ cup bread crumbs

¼ cup grated Parmesan cheese

¼ cup finely chopped fresh parsley

½ teaspoon dried oregano

1½ teaspoons salt

Freshly ground black pepper, to taste

2 eggs, lightly beaten

5 ounces (142 g) sharp or aged provolone cheese, cut into 1-inch cubes

1. Preheat a skillet over medium-high heat. Add the oil and cook the onion and garlic until tender, but not browned. 2. Transfer the onion and garlic to a large bowl and add the beef, pork, bread crumbs, Parmesan cheese, parsley, oregano, salt, pepper and eggs. Mix well until all the ingredients are combined. Divide the mixture into 12 evenly sized balls. Make one meatball at a time, by pressing a hole in the meatball mixture with the finger and pushing a piece of provolone cheese into the hole. Mold the meat back into a ball, enclosing the cheese. 3. Preheat the air fryer to 380ºF (193ºC). 4. Working in two batches, transfer six of the meatballs to the air fryer basket and air fry for 12 minutes, shaking the basket and turning the meatballs twice during the cooking process. Repeat with the remaining 6 meatballs. Serve warm.

Spicy Sirloin Tip Steak

Prep time: 25 minutes | Cook time: 12 to 18 minutes | Serves 4

2 tablespoons salsa
1 tablespoon minced chipotle pepper
1 tablespoon apple cider vinegar
1 teaspoon ground cumin
⅛ teaspoon freshly ground black pepper
⅛ teaspoon red pepper flakes
12 ounces (340 g) sirloin tip steak, cut into 4 pieces and gently pounded to about ⅓ inch thick
Cooking oil spray

1. In a small bowl, thoroughly mix the salsa, chipotle pepper, vinegar, cumin, black pepper, and red pepper flakes. Rub this mixture into both sides of each steak piece. Let stand for 15 minutes at room temperature. 2. Insert the crisper plate into the basket and place the basket into the unit. Preheat the unit by selecting AIR FRY, setting the temperature to 390ºF (199ºC), and setting the time to 3 minutes. Select START/STOP to begin. 3. Once the unit is preheated, spray the crisper plate with cooking oil. Working in batches, place 2 steaks into the basket. 4. Select AIR FRY, set the temperature to 390ºF (199ºC), and set the time to 9 minutes. Select START/STOP to begin. 5. After about 6 minutes, check the steaks. If a food thermometer inserted into the meat registers at least 145ºF (63ºC), they are done. If not, resume cooking. 6. When the cooking is done, transfer the steaks to a clean plate and cover with aluminum foil to keep warm. Repeat steps 3, 4, and 5 with the remaining steaks. 7. Thinly slice the steaks against the grain and serve.

Panko Crusted Calf's Liver Strips

Prep time: 15 minutes | Cook time: 23 to 25 minutes | Serves 4

1 pound (454 g) sliced calf's liver, cut into ½-inch wide strips
2 eggs
2 tablespoons milk
½ cup whole wheat flour
2 cups panko breadcrumbs
Salt and ground black pepper, to taste
Cooking spray

1. Preheat the air fryer to 390ºF (199ºC) and spritz with cooking spray. 2. Rub the calf's liver strips with salt and ground black pepper on a clean work surface. 3. Whisk the eggs with milk in a large bowl. Pour the flour in a shallow dish. Pour the panko on a separate shallow dish. 4. Dunk the liver strips in the flour, then in the egg mixture. Shake the excess off and roll the strips over the panko to coat well. 5. Arrange half of the liver strips in a single layer in the preheated air fryer and spritz with cooking spray. 6. Air fry for 5 minutes or until browned. Flip the strips halfway through. Repeat with the remaining strips. 7. Serve immediately.

Swedish Meatloaf

Prep time: 10 minutes | Cook time: 35 minutes | Serves 8

1½ pounds (680 g) ground beef (85% lean)
¼ pound (113 g) ground pork
1 large egg (omit for egg-free)
½ cup minced onions
¼ cup tomato sauce
2 tablespoons dry mustard
2 cloves garlic, minced
2 teaspoons fine sea salt
1 teaspoon ground black pepper, plus more for garnish

Sauce:
½ cup (1 stick) unsalted butter
½ cup shredded Swiss or mild Cheddar cheese (about 2 ounces / 57 g)
2 ounces (57 g) cream cheese (¼ cup), softened
⅓ cup beef broth
⅛ teaspoon ground nutmeg
Halved cherry tomatoes, for serving (optional)

1. Preheat the air fryer to 390ºF (199ºC). 2. In a large bowl, combine the ground beef, ground pork, egg, onions, tomato sauce, dry mustard, garlic, salt, and pepper. Using your hands, mix until well combined. 3. Place the meatloaf mixture in a loaf pan and place it in the air fryer. Bake for 35 minutes, or until cooked through and the internal temperature reaches 145ºF (63ºC). Check the meatloaf after 25 minutes; if it's getting too brown on the top, cover it loosely with foil to prevent burning. 4. While the meatloaf cooks, make the sauce: Heat the butter in a saucepan over medium-high heat until it sizzles and brown flecks appear, stirring constantly to keep the butter from burning. Turn the heat down to low and whisk in the Swiss cheese, cream cheese, broth, and nutmeg. Simmer for at least 10 minutes. The longer it simmers, the more the flavors open up. 5. When the meatloaf is done, transfer it to a serving tray and pour the sauce over it. Garnish with ground black pepper and serve with cherry tomatoes, if desired. Allow the meatloaf to rest for 10 minutes before slicing so it doesn't crumble apart. 6. Store leftovers in an airtight container in the fridge for 3 days or in the freezer for up to a month. Reheat in a preheated 350ºF (177ºC) air fryer for 4 minutes, or until heated through.

Dijon Porterhouse Steak

Prep time: 20 minutes | Cook time: 14 minutes | Serves 2

1 pound (454 g) porterhouse steak, cut meat from bones in 2 pieces
½ teaspoon ground black pepper
1 teaspoon cayenne pepper
½ teaspoon salt
1 teaspoon garlic powder
½ teaspoon dried thyme
½ teaspoon dried marjoram
1 teaspoon Dijon mustard
1 tablespoon butter, melted

1. Sprinkle the porterhouse steak with all the seasonings. 2. Spread the mustard and butter evenly over the meat. 3. Cook in the preheated air fryer at 390ºF (199ºC) for 12 to 14 minutes. 4. Taste for doneness with a meat thermometer and serve immediately.

Herb-Roasted Beef Tips with Onions

Prep time: 5 minutes | Cook time: 10 minutes | Serves 4

1 pound (454 g) rib eye steak, cubed	1 tablespoon fresh oregano
2 garlic cloves, minced	1 teaspoon salt
2 tablespoons olive oil	½ teaspoon black pepper
	1 yellow onion, thinly sliced

1. Preheat the air fryer to 380°F(193°C). 2. In a medium bowl, combine the steak, garlic, olive oil, oregano, salt, pepper, and onion. Mix until all of the beef and onion are well coated. 3. Put the seasoned steak mixture into the air fryer basket. Roast for 5 minutes. Stir and roast for 5 minutes more. 4. Let rest for 5 minutes before serving with some favorite sides.

Chuck Kebab with Arugula

Prep time: 30 minutes | Cook time: 25 minutes | Serves 4

½ cup leeks, chopped	½ teaspoon ground sumac
2 garlic cloves, smashed	3 saffron threads
2 pounds (907 g) ground chuck	2 tablespoons loosely packed
Salt, to taste	fresh continental parsley leaves
¼ teaspoon ground black pepper, or more to taste	4 tablespoons tahini sauce
	4 ounces (113 g) baby arugula
1 teaspoon cayenne pepper	1 tomato, cut into slices

1. In a bowl, mix the chopped leeks, garlic, ground chuck, and spices; knead with your hands until everything is well incorporated. 2. Now, mound the beef mixture around a wooden skewer into a pointed-ended sausage. 3. Cook in the preheated air fryer at 360°F (182°C) for 25 minutes. Serve your kebab with the tahini sauce, baby arugula and tomato. Enjoy!

Reuben Beef Rolls with Thousand Island Sauce

Prep time: 15 minutes | Cook time: 10 minutes per batch | Makes 10 rolls

½ pound (227 g) cooked corned beef, chopped	Thousand Island Sauce:
½ cup drained and chopped sauerkraut	¼ cup chopped dill pickles
	¼ cup tomato sauce
1 (8-ounce / 227-g) package cream cheese, softened	¾ cup mayonnaise
	Fresh thyme leaves, for garnish
½ cup shredded Swiss cheese	2 tablespoons sugar
20 slices prosciutto	⅛ teaspoon fine sea salt
Cooking spray	Ground black pepper, to taste

1. Preheat the air fryer to 400°F (204°C) and spritz with cooking spray. 2. Combine the beef, sauerkraut, cream cheese, and Swiss cheese in a large bowl. Stir to mix well. 3. Unroll a slice of prosciutto on a clean work surface, then top with another slice of prosciutto crosswise. Scoop up 4 tablespoons of the beef mixture in the center. 4. Fold the top slice sides over the filling as the ends of the roll, then roll up the long sides of the bottom prosciutto and make it into a roll shape. Overlap the sides by about 1 inch. Repeat with remaining filling and prosciutto. 5. Arrange the rolls in the preheated air fryer, seam side down, and spritz with cooking spray. 6. Air fry for 10 minutes or until golden and crispy. Flip the rolls halfway through. Work in batches to avoid overcrowding. 7. Meanwhile, combine the ingredients for the sauce in a small bowl. Stir to mix well. 8. Serve the rolls with the dipping sauce.

Caraway Crusted Beef Steaks

Prep time: 5 minutes | Cook time: 10 minutes | Serves 4

4 beef steaks	taste
2 teaspoons caraway seeds	1 tablespoon melted butter
2 teaspoons garlic powder	⅓ cup almond flour
Sea salt and cayenne pepper, to	2 eggs, beaten

1. Preheat the air fryer to 355°F (179°C). 2. Add the beef steaks to a large bowl and toss with the caraway seeds, garlic powder, salt and pepper until well coated. 3. Stir together the melted butter and almond flour in a bowl. Whisk the eggs in a different bowl. 4. Dredge the seasoned steaks in the eggs, then dip in the almond and butter mixture. 5. Arrange the coated steaks in the air fryer basket. Air fryer for 10 minutes, or until the internal temperature of the beef steaks reaches at least 145°F (63°C) on a meat thermometer. Flip the steaks once halfway through to ensure even cooking. 6. Transfer the steaks to plates. Let cool for 5 minutes and serve hot.

New York Strip with Honey-Mustard Butter

Prep time: 5 minutes | Cook time: 14 minutes | Serves 4

2 pounds (907 g) New York Strip	½ stick butter, softened
1 teaspoon cayenne pepper	Sea salt and freshly ground black pepper, to taste
1 tablespoon honey	Cooking spray
1 tablespoon Dijon mustard	

1. Preheat the air fryer to 400°F (204°C) and spritz with cooking spray. 2. Sprinkle the New York Strip with cayenne pepper, salt, and black pepper on a clean work surface. 3. Arrange the New York Strip in the preheated air fryer and spritz with cooking spray. 4. Air fry for 14 minutes or until browned and reach your desired doneness. Flip the New York Strip halfway through. 5. Meanwhile, combine the honey, mustard, and butter in a small bowl. Stir to mix well. 6. Transfer the air fried New York Strip onto a plate and baste with the honey-mustard butter before serving.

Meat and Rice Stuffed Bell Peppers

Prep time: 20 minutes | Cook time: 18 minutes | Serves 4

¾ pound (340 g) lean ground beef
4 ounces (113 g) lean ground pork
¼ cup onion, minced
1 (15-ounce / 425-g) can crushed tomatoes
1 teaspoon Worcestershire sauce
1 teaspoon barbecue seasoning

1 teaspoon honey
½ teaspoon dried basil
½ cup cooked brown rice
½ teaspoon garlic powder
½ teaspoon oregano
½ teaspoon salt
2 small bell peppers, cut in half, stems removed, deseeded
Cooking spray

1. Preheat the air fryer to 360ºF (182ºC) and spritz a baking pan with cooking spray. 2. Arrange the beef, pork, and onion in the baking pan and bake in the preheated air fryer for 8 minutes. Break the ground meat into chunks halfway through the cooking. 3. Meanwhile, combine the tomatoes, Worcestershire sauce, barbecue seasoning, honey, and basil in a saucepan. Stir to mix well. 4. Transfer the cooked meat mixture to a large bowl and add the cooked rice, garlic powder, oregano, salt, and ¼ cup of the tomato mixture. Stir to mix well. 5. Stuff the pepper halves with the mixture, then arrange the pepper halves in the air fryer and air fry for 10 minutes or until the peppers are lightly charred. 6. Serve the stuffed peppers with the remaining tomato sauce on top.

Mojito Lamb Chops

Prep time: 30 minutes | Cook time: 5 minutes | Serves 2

Marinade:
2 teaspoons grated lime zest
½ cup lime juice
¼ cup avocado oil
¼ cup chopped fresh mint leaves
4 cloves garlic, roughly chopped

2 teaspoons fine sea salt
½ teaspoon ground black pepper
4 (1-inch-thick) lamb chops
Sprigs of fresh mint, for garnish (optional)
Lime slices, for serving (optional)

1. Make the marinade: Place all the ingredients for the marinade in a food processor or blender and purée until mostly smooth with a few small chunks. Transfer half of the marinade to a shallow dish and set the other half aside for serving. Add the lamb to the shallow dish, cover, and place in the refrigerator to marinate for at least 2 hours or overnight. 2. Spray the air fryer basket with avocado oil. Preheat the air fryer to 390ºF (199ºC). 3. Remove the chops from the marinade and place them in the air fryer basket. Air fry for 5 minutes, or until the internal temperature reaches 145ºF (63ºC) for medium doneness. 4. Allow the chops to rest for 10 minutes before serving with the rest of the marinade as a sauce. Garnish with fresh mint leaves and serve with lime slices, if desired. Best served fresh.

Italian Steak Rolls

Prep time: 30 minutes | Cook time: 9 minutes | Serves 4

1 tablespoon vegetable oil
2 cloves garlic, minced
2 teaspoons dried Italian seasoning
1 teaspoon kosher salt
1 teaspoon black pepper
1 pound (454 g) flank or skirt steak, ¼ to ½ inch thick

1 (10-ounce / 283-g) package frozen spinach, thawed and squeezed dry
½ cup diced jarred roasted red pepper
1 cup shredded Mozzarella cheese

1. In a large bowl, combine the oil, garlic, Italian seasoning, salt, and pepper. Whisk to combine. Add the steak to the bowl, turning to ensure the entire steak is covered with the seasonings. Cover and marinate at room temperature for 30 minutes or in the refrigerator for up to 24 hours. 2. Lay the steak on a flat surface. Spread the spinach evenly over the steak, leaving a ¼-inch border at the edge. Evenly top each steak with the red pepper and cheese. 3. Starting at a long end, roll up the steak as tightly as possible, ending seam side down. Use 2 or 3 wooden toothpicks to hold the roll together. Using a sharp knife, cut the roll in half so that it better fits in the air fryer basket. 4. Place the steak roll, seam side down, in the air fryer basket. Set the air fryer to 400ºF (204ºC) for 9 minutes. Use a meat thermometer to ensure the steak has reached an internal temperature of 145ºF (63ºC). (It is critical to not overcook flank steak, so as to not toughen the meat.) 5. Let the steak rest for 10 minutes before cutting into slices to serve.

Cheese Pork Chops

Prep time: 15 minutes | Cook time: 9 to 14 minutes | Serves 4

2 large eggs
½ cup finely grated Parmesan cheese
½ cup finely ground blanched almond flour or finely crushed pork rinds
1 teaspoon paprika

½ teaspoon dried oregano
½ teaspoon garlic powder
Salt and freshly ground black pepper, to taste
1¼ pounds (567 g) (1-inch-thick) boneless pork chops
Avocado oil spray

1. Beat the eggs in a shallow bowl. In a separate bowl, combine the Parmesan cheese, almond flour, paprika, oregano, garlic powder, and salt and pepper to taste. 2. Dip the pork chops into the eggs, then coat them with the Parmesan mixture, gently pressing the coating onto the meat. Spray the breaded pork chops with oil. 3. Set the air fryer to 400ºF (204ºC). Place the pork chops in the air fryer basket in a single layer, working in batches if necessary. Cook for 6 minutes. Flip the chops and spray them with more oil. Cook for another 3 to 8 minutes, until an instant-read thermometer reads 145ºF (63ºC). 4. Allow the pork chops to rest for at least 5 minutes, then serve.

Parmesan Herb Filet Mignon

Prep time: 20 minutes | Cook time: 13 minutes | Serves 4

1 pound (454 g) filet mignon	1 teaspoon dried rosemary
Sea salt and ground black	1 teaspoon dried thyme
pepper, to taste	1 tablespoon sesame oil
½ teaspoon cayenne pepper	1 small-sized egg, well-whisked
1 teaspoon dried basil	½ cup Parmesan cheese, grated

1. Season the filet mignon with salt, black pepper, cayenne pepper, basil, rosemary, and thyme. Brush with sesame oil. 2. Put the egg in a shallow plate. Now, place the Parmesan cheese in another plate. 3. Coat the filet mignon with the egg; then lay it into the Parmesan cheese. Set the air fryer to 360ºF (182ºC). 4. Cook for 10 to 13 minutes or until golden. Serve with mixed salad leaves and enjoy!

Herbed Lamb Steaks

Prep time: 30 minutes | Cook time: 15 minutes | Serves 4

½ medium onion	1 teaspoon cayenne pepper
2 tablespoons minced garlic	1 teaspoon salt
2 teaspoons ground ginger	4 (6-ounce / 170-g) boneless
1 teaspoon ground cinnamon	lamb sirloin steaks
1 teaspoon onion powder	Oil, for spraying

1. In a blender, combine the onion, garlic, ginger, cinnamon, onion powder, cayenne pepper, and salt and pulse until the onion is minced. 2. Place the lamb steaks in a large bowl or zip-top plastic bag and sprinkle the onion mixture over the top. Turn the steaks until they are evenly coated. Cover with plastic wrap or seal the bag and refrigerate for 30 minutes. 3. Preheat the air fryer to 330ºF (166ºC). Line the air fryer basket with parchment and spray lightly with oil. 4. Place the lamb steaks in a single layer in the prepared basket, making sure they don't overlap. You may need to work in batches, depending on the size of your air fryer. 5. Cook for 8 minutes, flip, and cook for another 7 minutes, or until the internal temperature reaches 155ºF (68ºC).

Spice-Rubbed Pork Loin

Prep time: 5 minutes | Cook time: 20 minutes | Serves 6

1 teaspoon paprika	1 (1½-pound / 680-g) boneless
½ teaspoon ground cumin	pork loin
½ teaspoon chili powder	½ teaspoon salt
½ teaspoon garlic powder	¼ teaspoon ground black
2 tablespoons coconut oil	pepper

1. In a small bowl, mix paprika, cumin, chili powder, and garlic powder. 2. Drizzle coconut oil over pork. Sprinkle pork loin with salt and pepper, then rub spice mixture evenly on all sides. 3. Place pork loin into ungreased air fryer basket. Adjust the temperature

to 400ºF (204ºC) and air fry for 20 minutes, turning pork halfway through cooking. Pork loin will be browned and have an internal temperature of at least 145ºF (63ºC) when done. Serve warm.

Peppercorn-Crusted Beef Tenderloin

Prep time: 10 minutes | Cook time: 25 minutes | Serves 6

2 tablespoons salted butter,	4-peppercorn blend
melted	1 (2-pound / 907-g) beef
2 teaspoons minced roasted	tenderloin, trimmed of visible
garlic	fat
3 tablespoons ground	

1. In a small bowl, mix the butter and roasted garlic. Brush it over the beef tenderloin. 2. Place the ground peppercorns onto a plate and roll the tenderloin through them, creating a crust. Place tenderloin into the air fryer basket. 3. Adjust the temperature to 400ºF (204ºC) and roast for 25 minutes. 4. Turn the tenderloin halfway through the cooking time. 5. Allow meat to rest 10 minutes before slicing.

Beefy Poppers

Prep time: 15 minutes | Cook time: 15 minutes |
Makes 8 poppers

8 medium jalapeño peppers,	(85% lean)
stemmed, halved, and seeded	1 teaspoon fine sea salt
1 (8-ounce / 227-g) package	½ teaspoon ground black
cream cheese (or Kite Hill	pepper
brand cream cheese style spread	8 slices thin-cut bacon
for dairy-free), softened	Fresh cilantro leaves, for
2 pounds (907 g) ground beef	garnish

1. Spray the air fryer basket with avocado oil. Preheat the air fryer to 400ºF (204ºC). 2. Stuff each jalapeño half with a few tablespoons of cream cheese. Place the halves back together again to form 8 jalapeños. 3. Season the ground beef with the salt and pepper and mix with your hands to incorporate. Flatten about ¼ pound (113 g) of ground beef in the palm of your hand and place a stuffed jalapeño in the center. Fold the beef around the jalapeño, forming an egg shape. Wrap the beef-covered jalapeño with a slice of bacon and secure it with a toothpick. 4. Place the jalapeños in the air fryer basket, leaving space between them (if you're using a smaller air fryer, work in batches if necessary), and air fry for 15 minutes, or until the beef is cooked through and the bacon is crispy. Garnish with cilantro before serving. 5. Store leftovers in an airtight container in the fridge for 3 days or in the freezer for up to a month. Reheat in a preheated 350ºF (177ºC) air fryer for 4 minutes, or until heated through and the bacon is crispy.

Ground Beef Taco Rolls

Prep time: 20 minutes | Cook time: 10 minutes | Serves 4

½ pound (227 g) 80/20 ground beef
⅓ cup water
1 tablespoon chili powder
2 teaspoons cumin
½ teaspoon garlic powder
¼ teaspoon dried oregano
¼ cup canned diced tomatoes

and chiles, drained
2 tablespoons chopped cilantro
1½ cups shredded Mozzarella cheese
½ cup blanched finely ground almond flour
2 ounces (57 g) full-fat cream cheese
1 large egg

1. In a medium skillet over medium heat, brown the ground beef about 7 to 10 minutes. When meat is fully cooked, drain. 2. Add water to skillet and stir in chili powder, cumin, garlic powder, oregano, and tomatoes with chiles. Add cilantro. Bring to a boil, then reduce heat to simmer for 3 minutes. 3. In a large microwave-safe bowl, place Mozzarella, almond flour, cream cheese, and egg. Microwave for 1 minute. Stir the mixture quickly until smooth ball of dough forms. 4. Cut a piece of parchment for your work surface. Press the dough into a large rectangle on the parchment, wetting your hands to prevent the dough from sticking as necessary. Cut the dough into eight rectangles. 5. On each rectangle place a few spoons of the meat mixture. Fold the short ends of each roll toward the center and roll the length as you would a burrito. 6. Cut a piece of parchment to fit your air fryer basket. Place taco rolls onto the parchment and place into the air fryer basket. 7. Adjust the temperature to 360ºF (182ºC) and air fry for 10 minutes. 8. Flip halfway through the cooking time. 9. Allow to cool 10 minutes before serving.

Mustard and Rosemary Pork Tenderloin

Prep time: 10 minutes | Cook time: 26 minutes | Serves 2 to 3

1 pork tenderloin (about 1 pound / 454 g)
2 tablespoons coarse brown mustard
Salt and freshly ground black pepper, to taste

1½ teaspoons finely chopped fresh rosemary, plus sprigs for garnish
2 apples, cored and cut into 8 wedges
1 tablespoon butter, melted
1 teaspoon brown sugar

1. Preheat the air fryer to 370ºF (188ºC). 2. Cut the pork tenderloin in half so that you have two pieces that fit into the air fryer basket. Brush the mustard onto both halves of the pork tenderloin and then season with salt, pepper and the fresh rosemary. Place the pork tenderloin halves into the air fryer basket and air fry for 10 minutes. Turn the pork over and air fry for an additional 5 to 8 minutes or until the internal temperature of the pork registers 155ºF (68ºC) on an instant read thermometer. If your pork tenderloin is especially thick, you may need to add a minute or two, but it's better to check the pork and add time, than to overcook it. 3. Let the pork rest for 5 minutes. In the meantime, toss the apple wedges with the butter and

brown sugar and air fry at 400ºF (204ºC) for 8 minutes, shaking the basket once or twice during the cooking process so the apples cook and brown evenly. 4. Slice the pork on the bias. Serve with the fried apples scattered over the top and a few sprigs of rosemary as garnish.

Panko Pork Chops

Prep time: 10 minutes | Cook time: 12 minutes | Serves 4

4 center-cut boneless pork chops, excess fat trimmed
¼ teaspoon salt
2 eggs
1½ cups panko bread crumbs
3 tablespoons grated Parmesan cheese

1½ teaspoons paprika
½ teaspoon granulated garlic
½ teaspoon onion powder
1 teaspoon chili powder
¼ teaspoon freshly ground black pepper
Olive oil spray

1. Sprinkle the pork chops with salt on both sides and let them sit while you prepare the seasonings and egg wash. 2. In a shallow medium bowl, beat the eggs. 3. In another shallow medium bowl, stir together the panko, Parmesan cheese, paprika, granulated garlic, onion powder, chili powder, and pepper. 4. Dip the pork chops in the egg and in the panko mixture to coat. Firmly press the crumbs onto the chops. 5. Insert the crisper plate into the basket and the basket into the unit. Preheat the unit by selecting AIR ROAST, setting the temperature to 400ºF (204ºC), and setting the time to 3 minutes. Select START/STOP to begin. 6. Once the unit is preheated, spray the crisper plate with olive oil. Place the pork chops into the basket and spray them with olive oil. 7. Select AIR ROAST, set the temperature to 400ºF (204ºC), and set the time to 12 minutes. Select START/STOP to begin. 8. After 6 minutes, flip the pork chops and spray them with more olive oil. Resume cooking. 9. When the cooking is complete, the chops should be golden and crispy and a food thermometer should register 145ºF (63ºC). Serve immediately.

Simple Ground Beef with Zucchini

Prep time: 5 minutes | Cook time: 12 minutes | Serves 4

1½ pounds (680 g) ground beef
1 pound (454 g) chopped zucchini
2 tablespoons extra-virgin olive oil

1 teaspoon dried oregano
1 teaspoon dried basil
1 teaspoon dried rosemary
2 tablespoons fresh chives, chopped

1. Preheat the air fryer to 400ºF (204ºC). 2. In a large bowl, combine all the ingredients, except for the chives, until well blended. 3. Place the beef and zucchini mixture in the baking pan. Air fry for 12 minutes, or until the beef is browned and the zucchini is tender. 4. Divide the beef and zucchini mixture among four serving dishes. Top with fresh chives and serve hot.

Chapter 4 Fish and Seafood

16

Lemony Salmon

Prep time: 30 minutes | Cook time: 10 minutes | Serves 4

1½ pounds (680 g) salmon steak	Fresh chopped chives, for garnish
½ teaspoon grated lemon zest	½ cup dry white wine
Freshly cracked mixed peppercorns, to taste	½ teaspoon fresh cilantro, chopped
⅓ cup lemon juice	Fine sea salt, to taste

1. To prepare the marinade, place all ingredients, except for salmon steak and chives, in a deep pan. Bring to a boil over medium-high flame until it has reduced by half. Allow it to cool down. 2. After that, allow salmon steak to marinate in the refrigerator approximately 40 minutes. Discard the marinade and transfer the fish steak to the preheated air fryer. 3. Air fry at 400ºF (204ºC) for 9 to 10 minutes. To finish, brush hot fish steaks with the reserved marinade, garnish with fresh chopped chives, and serve right away!

Tuna-Stuffed Quinoa Patties

Prep time: 10 minutes | Cook time: 15 minutes | Serves 4

12 ounces (340 g) quinoa	in olive oil, drained
4 slices white bread with crusts removed	2 to 3 lemons
	Kosher salt and pepper, to taste
½ cup milk	1¼ cups panko bread crumbs
3 eggs	Vegetable oil, for spraying
10 ounces (283 g) tuna packed	Lemon wedges, for serving

1. Rinse the quinoa in a fine-mesh sieve until the water runs clear. Bring 4 cups of salted water to a boil. Add the quinoa, cover, and reduce heat to low. Simmer the quinoa covered until most of the water is absorbed and the quinoa is tender, 15 to 20 minutes. Drain and allow to cool to room temperature. Meanwhile, soak the bread in the milk. 2. Mix the drained quinoa with the soaked bread and 2 of the eggs in a large bowl and mix thoroughly. In a medium bowl, combine the tuna, the remaining egg, and the juice and zest of 1 of the lemons. Season well with salt and pepper. Spread the panko on a plate. 3. Scoop up approximately ½ cup of the quinoa mixture and flatten into a patty. Place a heaping tablespoon of the tuna mixture in the center of the patty and close the quinoa around the tuna. Flatten the patty slightly to create an oval-shaped croquette. Dredge both sides of the croquette in the panko. Repeat with the remaining quinoa and tuna. 4. Spray the air fryer basket with oil to prevent sticking, and preheat the air fryer to 400ºF (204ºC). Arrange 4 or 5 of the croquettes in the basket, taking care to avoid overcrowding. Spray the tops of the croquettes with oil. Air fry for 8 minutes until the top side is browned and crispy. Carefully turn the croquettes over and spray the second side with oil. Air fry until the second side is browned and crispy, another 7 minutes. Repeat with the remaining croquettes. 5. Serve the croquetas warm with plenty of lemon wedges for spritzing.

Crab Cakes

Prep time: 10 minutes | Cook time: 10 minutes | Serves 4

2 (6-ounce / 170-g) cans lump crab meat

¼ cup blanched finely ground almond flour

1 large egg

2 tablespoons full-fat mayonnaise

½ teaspoon Dijon mustard

½ tablespoon lemon juice

½ medium green bell pepper, seeded and chopped

¼ cup chopped green onion

½ teaspoon Old Bay seasoning

1. In a large bowl, combine all ingredients. Form into four balls and flatten into patties. Place patties into the air fryer basket. 2. Adjust the temperature to 350°F (177°C) and air fry for 10 minutes. 3. Flip patties halfway through the cooking time. Serve warm.

Southern-Style Catfish

Prep time: 10 minutes | Cook time: 12 minutes | Serves 4

4 (7-ounce / 198-g) catfish fillets

⅓ cup heavy whipping cream

1 tablespoon lemon juice

1 cup blanched finely ground

almond flour

2 teaspoons Old Bay seasoning

½ teaspoon salt

¼ teaspoon ground black pepper

1. Place catfish fillets into a large bowl with cream and pour in lemon juice. Stir to coat. 2. In a separate large bowl, mix flour and Old Bay seasoning. 3. Remove each fillet and gently shake off excess cream. Sprinkle with salt and pepper. Press each fillet gently into flour mixture on both sides to coat. 4. Place fillets into ungreased air fryer basket. Adjust the temperature to 400°F (204°C) and air fry for 12 minutes, turning fillets halfway through cooking. Catfish will be golden brown and have an internal temperature of at least 145°F (63°C) when done. Serve warm.

Catfish Bites

Prep time: 15 minutes | Cook time: 20 minutes | Serves 4

Oil, for spraying	2 teaspoons Creole seasoning
1 pound (454 g) catfish fillets,	½ cup yellow mustard
cut into 2-inch pieces	½ cup salad sauce, for serving
1 cup buttermilk	1 cup fried fries, for serving
½ cup cornmeal	(optional)
¼ cup all-purpose flour	

Line the air fryer basket with parchment and spray lightly with oil. 2. Place the catfish pieces and buttermilk in a zip-top plastic bag, seal, and refrigerate for about 10 minutes. 3. In a shallow bowl, mix together the cornmeal, flour, and Creole seasoning. 4. Remove the catfish from the bag and pat dry with a paper towel. 5. Spread the mustard on all sides of the catfish, then dip them in the cornmeal mixture until evenly coated. 6. Place the catfish in the prepared basket. You may need to work in batches, depending on the size of your air fryer. Spray lightly with oil. 7. Air fry at 400ºF (204ºC) for 10 minutes, flip carefully, spray with oil, and cook for another 10 minutes. Serve immediately with salad sauce and fried fries.

Butter-Wine Baked Salmon

Prep time: 5 minutes | Cook time: 10 minutes | Serves 4

4 tablespoons butter, melted	1 teaspoon smoked paprika
2 cloves garlic, minced	½ teaspoon onion powder
Sea salt and ground black	4 salmon steaks
pepper, to taste	Cooking spray
¼ cup dry white wine	12 sprig of thyme, for garnish
1 tablespoon lime juice	

1. Place all the ingredients except the salmon and oil in a shallow dish and stir to mix well. 2. Add the salmon steaks, turning to coat well on both sides. Transfer the salmon to the refrigerator to marinate for 30 minutes. 3. Preheat the air fryer to 360ºF (182ºC). 4. Place the salmon steaks in the air fryer basket, discarding any excess marinade. Spray the salmon steaks with cooking spray. 5. Air fry for about 10 minutes, flipping the salmon steaks halfway through, or until cooked to your preferred doneness. 6. Divide the salmon steaks among four plates, garnish with thyme and serve.

Catfish Bites

Prep time: 15 minutes | Cook time: 20 minutes | Serves 4

Oil, for spraying
1 pound (454 g) catfish fillets, cut into 2-inch pieces
1 cup buttermilk
½ cup cornmeal
¼ cup all-purpose flour
2 teaspoons Creole seasoning
½ cup yellow mustard
½ cup salad sauce, for serving
1 cup fried fries, for serving (optional)

Line the air fryer basket with parchment and spray lightly with oil. 2. Place the catfish pieces and buttermilk in a zip-top plastic bag, seal, and refrigerate for about 10 minutes. 3. In a shallow bowl, mix together the cornmeal, flour, and Creole seasoning. 4. Remove the catfish from the bag and pat dry with a paper towel. 5. Spread the mustard on all sides of the catfish, then dip them in the cornmeal mixture until evenly coated. 6. Place the catfish in the prepared basket. You may need to work in batches, depending on the size of your air fryer. Spray lightly with oil. 7. Air fry at 400ºF (204ºC) for 10 minutes, flip carefully, spray with oil, and cook for another 10 minutes. Serve immediately with salad sauce and fried fries.

Air Fryer Fish Fry

Prep time: 5 minutes | Cook time: 15 minutes | Serves 4

2 cups low-fat buttermilk
½ teaspoon garlic powder
½ teaspoon onion powder
4 (4-ounce) flounder fillets
½ cup plain yellow cornmeal
½ cup chickpea flour
¼ teaspoon cayenne pepper
Freshly ground black pepper
½ lemon, for serving (optional)
1 cup fried fries, for serving (optional)

1. In a large bowl, combine the buttermilk, garlic powder, and onion powder. 2. Add the flounder, turning until well coated, and set aside to marinate for 20 minutes. 3. In a shallow bowl, stir the cornmeal, chickpea flour, cayenne, and pepper together. 4. Dredge the fillets in the meal mixture, turning until well coated. Place in the basket of an air fryer. 5. Set the air fryer to 380°F, close, and cook for 12 minutes. 6. Serve with lemon and fried fries, if desired.

Panko Catfish Nuggets

Prep time: 10 minutes | Cook time: 7 to 8 minutes | Serves 4

2 medium catfish fillets, cut into chunks (approximately 1 × 2 inch)
Salt and pepper, to taste
2 eggs
2 tablespoons skim milk
½ cup cornstarch
1 cup panko bread crumbs
Cooking spray

1. Preheat the air fryer to 390ºF (199ºC). 2. In a medium bowl, season the fish chunks with salt and pepper to taste. 3. In a small bowl, beat together the eggs with milk until well combined. 4. Place the cornstarch and bread crumbs into separate shallow dishes. 5. Dredge the fish chunks one at a time in the cornstarch, coating well on both sides, then dip in the egg mixture, shaking off any excess, finally press well into the bread crumbs. Spritz the fish chunks with cooking spray. 6. Arrange the fish chunks in the air fryer basket in a single layer. You may need to cook in batches depending on the size of your air fryer basket. 7. Fry the fish chunks for 7 to 8 minutes until they are no longer translucent in the center and golden brown. Shake the basket once during cooking. 8. Remove the fish chunks from the basket to a plate. Repeat with the remaining fish chunks. 9. Serve warm.

Shrimp Bake

Prep time: 15 minutes | Cook time: 5 minutes | Serves 4

14 ounces (397 g) shrimp, peeled
1 egg, beaten
½ lemon, for garnish
½ cup coconut milk
1 cup Cheddar cheese, shredded
½ teaspoon coconut oil

1. In the mixing bowl, mix shrimps with egg, coconut milk, Cheddar cheese, and coconut oil. 2. Then put the mixture in the baking ramekins and put in the air fryer. 3. Cook the shrimps at 400ºF (204ºC) for 5 minutes. 4. Serve with lemon.

Shrimp Kebabs

Prep time: 15 minutes | Cook time: 6 minutes | Serves 4

Oil, for spraying
1 pound (454 g) medium raw shrimp, peeled and deveined
4 tablespoons unsalted butter, melted
1 tablespoon Old Bay seasoning
1 tablespoon packed light brown sugar
1 tablespoon chopped fresh cilantro
1 teaspoon granulated garlic
1 teaspoon onion powder
½ teaspoon freshly ground black pepper
1 lime, for serving

1. Line the air fryer basket with parchment and spray lightly with oil. 2. Thread the shrimp onto the skewers and place them in the prepared basket. 3. In a small bowl, mix together the butter, Old Bay, brown sugar, garlic, onion powder, and black pepper. Brush the sauce on the shrimp. 4. Air fry at 400ºF (204ºC) for 5 to 6 minutes, or until pink and firm. Sprinkle with cilantro and serve with a lime immediately.

Golden Shrimp

Prep time: 20 minutes | Cook time: 7 minutes | Serves 4

2 egg whites
½ cup coconut flour
1 cup Parmigiano-Reggiano, grated
½ teaspoon celery seeds
½ teaspoon porcini powder
½ teaspoon onion powder
1 teaspoon garlic powder
½ teaspoon dried rosemary
½ teaspoon sea salt
½ teaspoon ground black pepper
1½ pounds (680 g) shrimp, deveined
1 lime, cut in half
1 sprig of parsley, for garnish

1. Whisk the egg with coconut flour and Parmigiano-Reggiano. Add in seasonings and mix to combine well. 2. Dip your shrimp in the batter. Roll until they are covered on all sides. 3. Cook in the preheated air fryer at 390ºF (199ºC) for 5 to 7 minutes or until golden brown. Work in batches. Garnish with parsley and serve with lime if desired.

Blackened Salmon

Prep time: 10 minutes | Cook time: 8 minutes | Serves 2

10 ounces (283 g) salmon fillet	1 teaspoon ground cumin
1 lemon, cut into quarters	1 teaspoon dried basil
¼ sliced tomato	1 tablespoon avocado oil
½ teaspoon ground coriander	2 sprig of thyme

1. In the shallow bowl, mix ground coriander, ground cumin, and dried basil. 2. Then coat the salmon fillet in the spices and sprinkle with avocado oil. 3. Put the fish in the air fryer basket and cook at 395ºF (202ºC) for 4 minutes per side. 4. Garnish with thyme and serve warm with tomato and lemon.

Miso Salmon

Prep time: 10 minutes | Cook time: 12 minutes | Serves 2

2 tablespoons brown sugar	black pepper
2 tablespoons soy sauce	1 (5-ounce / 142-g) salmon
2 tablespoons white miso paste	fillets
1 teaspoon minced garlic	4 ounces (113 g) asparagus
1 teaspoon minced fresh ginger	Vegetable oil spray
½ teaspoon freshly cracked	1 sprig of dill, for garnish

1. In a small bowl, whisk together the brown sugar, soy sauce, miso, garlic, ginger, and pepper to combine. 2. Place the salmon fillets and asparagus on a plate. Pour half the sauce over the fillets and asparagus ; turn the fillets to coat the other sides with sauce and stir the asparagus with sauce. 3. Spray the air fryer basket with vegetable oil spray. Place the sauce-covered salmon and asparagus in the basket. Set the air fryer to 400ºF (204ºC) for 12 minutes. Halfway through the cooking time, brush additional miso sauce on the salmon. 4. Garnish with the dill and serve.

and stir to combine. 5. Insert the crisper plate into the basket and the basket into the unit. Preheat the unit by selecting AIR FRY, setting the temperature to 400ºF (204ºC), and setting the time to 3 minutes. Select START/STOP to begin. 6. Remove the shrimp from the plastic bag. Dip each in the flour, the egg, and the bread crumbs to coat. Gently press the crumbs onto the shrimp. 7. Once the unit is preheated, spray the crisper plate and the basket with cooking oil. Place the shrimp in the basket. It is okay to stack them. Spray the shrimp with the cooking oil. 8. Select AIR FRY, set the temperature to 400ºF (204ºC), and set the time to 8 minutes. Select START/STOP to begin. 9. After 4 minutes, remove the basket and flip the shrimp one at a time. Reinsert the basket to resume cooking. 10. When the cooking is complete, the shrimp should be crisp. Let cool for 5 minutes and garnish with cilantro. Serve with cocktail sauce.

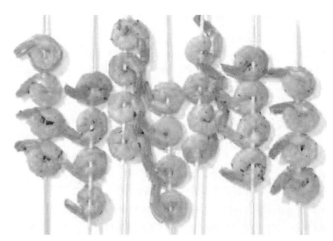

Cripsy Shrimp with Cilantro

Prep time: 40 minutes | Cook time: 10 minutes | Serves 4

1 pound (454 g) raw large shrimp, peeled and deveined with tails on or off	1 egg
	¾ cup bread crumbs
½ cup chopped fresh cilantro	Salt and freshly ground black pepper, to taste
Juice of 1 lime	Cooking oil spray
½ cup all-purpose flour	1 cup cocktail sauce

1. Place the shrimp in a resealable plastic bag and add the cilantro and lime juice. Seal the bag. Shake it to combine. Marinate the shrimp in the refrigerator for 30 minutes. 2. Place the flour in a small bowl. 3. In another small bowl, beat the egg. 4. Place the bread crumbs in a third small bowl, season with salt and pepper,

Quick Shrimp Skewers

Prep time: 10 minutes | Cook time: 5 minutes | Serves 5

4 pounds (1.8 kg) shrimp, peeled	1 tablespoon avocado oil
	1 teaspoon apple cider vinegar
1 tablespoon dried rosemary	

1. Mix the shrimps with dried rosemary, avocado oil, and apple cider vinegar. 2. Then sting the shrimps into skewers and put in the air fryer. 3. Cook the shrimps at 400ºF (204ºC) for 5 minutes.

Stuffed Flounder Florentine

Prep time: 10 minutes | Cook time: 25 minutes | Serves 4

¼ cup pine nuts
2 tablespoons olive oil
½ cup chopped tomatoes
1 (6-ounce / 170-g) bag spinach, coarsely chopped
2 cloves garlic, chopped
Salt and freshly ground black

pepper, to taste
2 tablespoons unsalted butter, divided
4 flounder fillets (about 1½ pounds / 680 g)
Dash of paprika
½ lemon, sliced into 4 wedges

1. Place the pine nuts in a baking dish that fits in your air fryer. Set the air fryer to 400ºF (204ºC) and air fry for 4 minutes until the nuts are lightly browned and fragrant. Remove the baking dish from the air fryer, tip the nuts onto a plate to cool, and continue preheating the air fryer. When the nuts are cool enough to handle, chop them into fine pieces. 2. In the baking dish, combine the oil, tomatoes, spinach, and garlic. Use tongs to toss until thoroughly combined. Air fry for 5 minutes until the tomatoes are softened and the spinach is wilted. 3. Transfer the vegetables to a bowl and stir in the toasted pine nuts. Season to taste with salt and freshly ground black pepper. 4. Place 1 tablespoon of the butter in the bottom of the baking dish. Lower the heat on the air fryer to 350ºF (177ºC). 5. Place the flounder on a clean work surface. Sprinkle both sides with salt and black pepper. Divide the vegetable mixture among the flounder fillets and carefully roll up, securing with toothpicks. 6. Working in batches if necessary, arrange the fillets seam-side down in the baking dish along with 1 tablespoon of water. Top the fillets with remaining 1 tablespoon butter and sprinkle with a dash of paprika. 7.Cover loosely with foil and air fry for 10 to 15 minutes until the fish is opaque and flakes easily with a fork. Remove the toothpicks before serving with the lemon wedges.

Chilean Sea Bass with Olive Relish

Prep time: 10 minutes | Cook time: 10 minutes | Serves 2

Olive oil spray
2 (6-ounce / 170-g) Chilean sea bass fillets or other firm-fleshed white fish
3 tablespoons extra-virgin olive oil

½ teaspoon ground cumin
½ teaspoon kosher salt
½ teaspoon black pepper
⅓ cup pitted green olives, diced
¼ cup finely diced onion
1 teaspoon chopped capers

1. Spray the air fryer basket with the olive oil spray. Drizzle the fillets with the olive oil and sprinkle with the cumin, salt, and pepper. Place the fish in the air fryer basket. Set the air fryer to 325ºF (163ºC) for 10 minutes, or until the fish flakes easily with a fork. 2. Meanwhile, in a small bowl, stir together the olives, onion, and capers. 3. Serve the fish topped with the relish.

Black Cod with Grapes and Kale

Prep time: 10 minutes | Cook time: 15 minutes | Serves 2

2 (6- to 8-ounce / 170- to 227-g) fillets of black cod
Salt and freshly ground black pepper, to taste
Olive oil
1 cup grapes, halved
1 small bulb fennel, sliced

¼-inch thick
½ cup pecans
3 cups shredded kale
2 teaspoons white balsamic vinegar or white wine vinegar
2 tablespoons extra-virgin olive oil

1. Preheat the air fryer to 400ºF (204ºC). 2. Season the cod fillets with salt and pepper and drizzle, brush or spray a little olive oil on top. Place the fish, presentation side up (skin side down), into the air fryer basket. Air fry for 10 minutes. 3. When the fish has finished cooking, remove the fillets to a side plate and loosely tent with foil to rest. 4. Toss the grapes, fennel and pecans in a bowl with a drizzle of olive oil and season with salt and pepper. Add the grapes, fennel and pecans to the air fryer basket and air fry for 5 minutes at 400ºF (204ºC), shaking the basket once during the cooking time. 5. Transfer the grapes, fennel and pecans to a bowl with the kale. Dress the kale with the balsamic vinegar and olive oil, season to taste with salt and pepper and serve along side the cooked fish.

Tandoori-Spiced Salmon and Potatoes

Prep time: 10 minutes | Cook time: 28 minutes | Serves 2

1 pound (454 g) fingerling potatoes
2 tablespoons vegetable oil, divided
Kosher salt and freshly ground black pepper, to taste
1 teaspoon ground turmeric

1 teaspoon ground cumin
1 teaspoon ground ginger
½ teaspoon smoked paprika
¼ teaspoon cayenne pepper
2 (6-ounce / 170-g) skin-on salmon fillets

1. Preheat the air fryer to 375ºF (191ºC). 2. In a bowl, toss the potatoes with 1 tablespoon of the oil until evenly coated. Season with salt and pepper. Transfer the potatoes to the air fryer and air fry for 20 minutes. 3. Meanwhile, in a bowl, combine the remaining 1 tablespoon oil, the turmeric, cumin, ginger, paprika, and cayenne. Add the salmon fillets and turn in the spice mixture until fully coated all over. 4. After the potatoes have cooked for 20 minutes, place the salmon fillets, skin-side up, on top of the potatoes, and continue cooking until the potatoes are tender, the salmon is cooked, and the salmon skin is slightly crisp. 5. Transfer the salmon fillets to two plates and serve with the potatoes while both are warm.

Cheesy Tuna Patties

Prep time: 5 minutes | Cook time: 17 to 18 minutes | Serves 4

Tuna Patties:	pepper, to taste
1 pound (454 g) canned tuna, drained	1 tablespoon sesame oil
	Cheese Sauce:
1 egg, whisked	1 tablespoon butter
2 tablespoons shallots, minced	1 cup beer
1 garlic clove, minced	2 tablespoons grated Colby
1 cup grated Romano cheese	cheese
Sea salt and ground black	

1. Mix together the canned tuna, whisked egg, shallots, garlic, cheese, salt, and pepper in a large bowl and stir to incorporate. 2. Divide the tuna mixture into four equal portions and form each portion into a patty with your hands. Refrigerate the patties for 2 hours. 3. When ready, brush both sides of each patty with sesame oil. 4. Preheat the air fryer to 360ºF (182ºC). 5. Place the patties in the air fryer basket and bake for 14 minutes, flipping the patties halfway through, or until lightly browned and cooked through. 6. Meanwhile, melt the butter in a pan over medium heat. 7. Pour in the beer and whisk constantly, or until it begins to bubble. 8. Add the grated Colby cheese and mix well. Continue cooking for 3 to 4 minutes, or until the cheese melts. Remove the patties from the basket to a plate. Drizzle them with the cheese sauce and serve immediately.

Salmon Spring Rolls

Prep time: 20 minutes | Cook time: 8 to 10 minutes | Serves 4

½ pound (227 g) salmon fillet	sliced
1 teaspoon toasted sesame oil	1 carrot, shredded
1 onion, sliced	⅓ cup chopped fresh flat-leaf
8 rice paper wrappers	parsley
1 yellow bell pepper, thinly	¼ cup chopped fresh basil

1. Put the salmon in the air fryer basket and drizzle with the sesame oil. Add the onion. Air fry at 370ºF (188ºC) for 8 to 10 minutes, or until the salmon just flakes when tested with a fork and the onion is tender. 2. Meanwhile, fill a small shallow bowl with warm water. One at a time, dip the rice paper wrappers into the water and place on a work surface. 3. Top each wrapper with one-eighth each of the salmon and onion mixture, yellow bell pepper, carrot, parsley, and basil. Roll up the wrapper, folding in the sides, to enclose the ingredients. 4. If you like, bake in the air fryer at 380ºF (193ºC) for 7 to 9 minutes, until the rolls are crunchy. Cut the rolls in half to serve.

Confetti Salmon Burgers

Prep time: 10 minutes | Cook time: 12 minutes | Serves 4

14 ounces (397 g) cooked fresh or canned salmon, flaked with a fork	1 teaspoon crab boil seasoning such as Old Bay
	½ teaspoon kosher salt
¼ cup minced scallion, white and light green parts only	½ teaspoon black pepper
	1 egg, beaten
¼ sliced tomato	½ cup fresh bread crumbs
¼ cup minced celery	Vegetable oil, for spraying
2 small lemons	

1. In a large bowl, combine the salmon, vegetables, the zest and juice of 1 of the lemons, crab boil seasoning, salt, and pepper. Add the egg and bread crumbs and stir to combine. Form the mixture into 4 patties weighing approximately 5 ounces (142 g) each. Chill until firm, about 15 minutes. 2. Preheat the air fryer to 400ºF (204ºC). 3. Spray the salmon patties with oil on all sides and spray the air fryer basket to prevent sticking. Air fry for 12 minutes, flipping halfway through, until the burgers are browned and cooked through. Cut the remaining lemon into 4 wedges and serve with the burgers.

Baked Salmon with Tomatoes and Olives

Prep time: 5 minutes | Cook time: 8 minutes | Serves 4

2 tablespoons olive oil	1 teaspoon chopped fresh dill
4 (1½-inch-thick) salmon fillets	2 Roma tomatoes, diced
½ teaspoon salt	¼ cup sliced Kalamata olives
¼ teaspoon cayenne	4 lemon slices

1. Preheat the air fryer to 380°F(193ºC). 2. Brush the olive oil on both sides of the salmon fillets, and then season them lightly with salt, cayenne, and dill. 3. Place the fillets in a single layer in the basket of the air fryer, then layer the tomatoes and olives over the top. Top each fillet with a lemon slice. 4. Bake for 8 minutes, or until the salmon has reached an internal temperature of 145°F(63ºC).

Salmon with Provolone Cheese

Prep time: 5 minutes | Cook time: 15 minutes | Serves 4

1 pound (454 g) salmon fillet, chopped	grated
	1 teaspoon avocado oil
2 ounces (57 g) Provolone,	¼ teaspoon ground paprika

1. Sprinkle the salmon fillets with avocado oil and put in the air fryer. 2. Then sprinkle the fish with ground paprika and top with Provolone cheese. 3. Cook the fish at 360ºF (182ºC) for 15 minutes.

Smoky Shrimp and Chorizo Tapas

Prep time: 15 minutes | Cook time: 10 minutes | Serves 2 to 4

4 ounces (113 g) Spanish (cured) chorizo, halved horizontally and sliced crosswise
½ pound (227 g) raw medium shrimp, peeled and deveined
1 tablespoon extra-virgin olive oil
1 small shallot, halved and thinly sliced

1 garlic clove, minced
1 tablespoon finely chopped fresh oregano
½ teaspoon smoked Spanish paprika
¼ teaspoon kosher salt
¼ teaspoon black pepper
3 tablespoons fresh orange juice
1 tablespoon minced fresh parsley

1. Place the chorizo in a baking pan. Set the pan in the air fryer basket. Set the air fryer to 375ºF (191ºC) for 5 minutes, or until the chorizo has started to brown and render its fat. 2. Meanwhile, in a large bowl, combine the shrimp, olive oil, shallot, garlic, oregano, paprika, salt, and pepper. Toss until the shrimp is well coated. 3. Transfer the shrimp to the pan with the chorizo. Stir to combine. Place the pan in the air fryer basket. Cook for 10 minutes, stirring halfway through the cooking time. 4. Transfer the shrimp and chorizo to a serving dish. Drizzle with the orange juice and toss to combine. Sprinkle with the parsley.

Jalea

Prep time: 20 minutes | Cook time: 10 minutes | Serves 4

Salsa Criolla:
½ red onion, thinly sliced
2 tomatoes, diced
1 serrano or jalapeño pepper, deseeded and diced
1 clove garlic, minced
¼ cup chopped fresh cilantro
Pinch of kosher salt
3 limes
Fried Seafood:
1 pound (454 g) firm, white-fleshed fish such as cod (add an extra ½-pound /227-g fish if not using shrimp)

20 large or jumbo shrimp, shelled and deveined
¼ cup all-purpose flour
¼ cup cornstarch
1 teaspoon garlic powder
1 teaspoon kosher salt
¼ teaspoon cayenne pepper
2 cups panko bread crumbs
2 eggs, beaten with 2 tablespoons water
Vegetable oil, for spraying
Mayonnaise or tartar sauce, for serving (optional)

1. To make the Salsa Criolla: combine the red onion, tomatoes, pepper, garlic, cilantro, and salt in a medium bowl. Add the juice and zest of 2 of the limes. Refrigerate the salad while you make the fish. 2. To make the seafood: cut the fish fillets into strips approximately 2 inches long and 1 inch wide. Place the flour, cornstarch, garlic powder, salt, and cayenne pepper on a plate and whisk to combine. Place the panko on a separate plate. Dredge the fish strips in the seasoned flour mixture, shaking off any excess. Dip the strips in the egg mixture, coating them completely, then dredge in the panko, shaking off any excess. Place the fish strips on a plate or rack. Repeat with the shrimp, if using. 3. Spray the air fryer basket with oil, and preheat the air fryer to 400ºF (204ºC). Working in 2 or 3 batches, arrange the fish and shrimp in a single layer in the basket, taking care not to crowd the basket. Spray with oil. Air fry for 5 minutes, then flip and air fry for another 4 to 5 minutes until the outside is brown and crisp and the inside of the fish is opaque and flakes easily with a fork. Repeat with the remaining seafood. 4. Place the fried seafood on a platter. Use a slotted spoon to remove the salsa criolla from the bowl, leaving behind any liquid that has accumulated. Place the salsa criolla on top of the fried seafood. Serve immediately with the remaining lime, cut into wedges, and mayonnaise or tartar sauce as desired.

Parmesan-Crusted Halibut Fillets

Prep time: 5 minutes | Cook time: 10 minutes | Serves 4

2 medium-sized halibut fillets
Dash of tabasco sauce
1 teaspoon curry powder
½ teaspoon ground coriander
½ teaspoon hot paprika

Kosher salt and freshly cracked mixed peppercorns, to taste
2 eggs
1½ tablespoons olive oil
½ cup grated Parmesan cheese

1. Preheat the air fryer to 365ºF (185ºC). 2. On a clean work surface, drizzle the halibut fillets with the tabasco sauce. Sprinkle with the curry powder, coriander, hot paprika, salt, and cracked mixed peppercorns. Set aside. 3. In a shallow bowl, beat the eggs until frothy. In another shallow bowl, combine the olive oil and Parmesan cheese. 4. One at a time, dredge the halibut fillets in the beaten eggs, shaking off any excess, then roll them over the Parmesan cheese until evenly coated. 5. Arrange the halibut fillets in the air fryer basket in a single layer and air fry for 10 minutes, or until the fish is golden brown and crisp. 6. Cool for 5 minutes before serving.

Honey-Balsamic Salmon

Prep time: 5 minutes | Cook time: 8 minutes | Serves 2

Oil, for spraying
2 (6-ounce / 170-g) salmon fillets
¼ cup balsamic vinegar
2 tablespoons honey

2 teaspoons red pepper flakes
2 teaspoons olive oil
½ teaspoon salt
¼ teaspoon freshly ground black pepper

1. Line the air fryer basket with parchment and spray lightly with oil. 2. Place the salmon in the prepared basket. 3. In a small bowl, whisk together the balsamic vinegar, honey, red pepper flakes, olive oil, salt, and black pepper. Brush the mixture over the salmon. 4. Roast at 390ºF (199ºC) for 7 to 8 minutes, or until the internal temperature reaches 145ºF (63ºC). Serve immediately.

Sea Bass with Potato Scales

Prep time: 10 minutes | Cook time: 10 minutes | Serves 2

2 (6- to 8-ounce / 170- to 227-
g) fillets of sea bass
Salt and freshly ground black
pepper, to taste
¼ cup mayonnaise
2 teaspoons finely chopped
lemon zest
1 teaspoon chopped fresh thyme
2 Fingerling potatoes, very

thinly sliced into rounds
Olive oil
½ clove garlic, crushed into a
paste
1 tablespoon capers, drained
and rinsed
1 tablespoon olive oil
1 teaspoon lemon juice, to taste

Preheat the air fryer to 400ºF (204ºC). 2. Season the fish well with salt and freshly ground black pepper. Mix the mayonnaise, lemon zest and thyme together in a small bowl. Spread a thin layer of the mayonnaise mixture on both fillets. Start layering rows of potato slices onto the fish fillets to simulate the fish scales. The second row should overlap the first row slightly. Dabbing a little more mayonnaise along the upper edge of the row of potatoes where the next row overlaps will help the potato slices stick. Press the potatoes onto the fish to secure them well and season again with salt. Brush or spray the potato layer with olive oil. 3. Transfer the fish to the air fryer and air fry for 8 to 10 minutes, depending on the thickness of your fillets. 1-inch of fish should take 10 minutes at 400ºF (204ºC). 4. While the fish is cooking, add the garlic, capers, olive oil and lemon juice to the remaining mayonnaise mixture to make the caper aïoli. 5. Serve the fish warm with a dollop of the aïoli on top or on the side.

Pecan-Crusted Tilapia

Prep time: 10minutes | Cook time: 10 minutes | Serves 4

1¼ cups pecans
¾ cup panko bread crumbs
½ cup all-purpose flour
2 tablespoons Cajun seasoning
2 eggs, beaten with 2

tablespoons water
4 (6-ounce/ 170-g) tilapia fillets
Vegetable oil, for spraying
Lemon wedges, for serving

Grind the pecans in the food processor until they resemble coarse meal. Combine the ground pecans with the panko on a plate. On a second plate, combine the flour and Cajun seasoning. Dry the tilapia fillets using paper towels and dredge them in the flour mixture, shaking off any excess. Dip the fillets in the egg mixture and then dredge them in the pecan and panko mixture, pressing the coating onto the fillets. Place the breaded fillets on a plate or rack. 2. Preheat the air fryer to 375ºF (191ºC). Spray both sides of the breaded fillets with oil. Carefully transfer 2 of the fillets to the air fryer basket and air fry for 9 to 10 minutes, flipping once halfway through, until the flesh is opaque and flaky. Repeat with the remaining fillets. 3. Serve immediately with lemon wedges.

Crab Cake Sandwich

Prep time: 15 minutes | Cook time: 10 minutes | Serves 4

Crab Cakes:
½ cup panko bread crumbs
1 large egg, beaten
1 large egg white
1 tablespoon mayonnaise
1 teaspoon Dijon mustard
¼ cup minced fresh parsley
1 tablespoon fresh lemon juice
½ teaspoon Old Bay seasoning
⅛ teaspoon sweet paprika
⅛ teaspoon kosher salt
Freshly ground black pepper, to
taste

10 ounces (283 g) lump crab
meat
Cooking spray
Cajun Mayo:
¼ cup mayonnaise
1 tablespoon minced dill pickle
1 teaspoon fresh lemon juice
¾ teaspoon Cajun seasoning
For Serving:
4 Boston lettuce leaves
4 whole wheat potato buns or
gluten-free buns

For the crab cakes: In a large bowl, combine the panko, whole egg, egg white, mayonnaise, mustard, parsley, lemon juice, Old Bay, paprika, salt, and pepper to taste and mix well. Fold in the crab meat, being careful not to over mix. Gently shape into 4 round patties, about ½ cup each, ¾ inch thick. Spray both sides with oil. 2. Preheat the air fryer to 370ºF (188ºC). 3. Working in batches, place the crab cakes in the air fryer basket. Air fry for about 10 minutes, flipping halfway, until the edges are golden. 4. Meanwhile, for the Cajun mayo: In a small bowl, combine the mayonnaise, pickle, lemon juice, and Cajun seasoning. 5. To serve: Place a lettuce leaf on each bun bottom and top with a crab cake and a generous tablespoon of Cajun mayonnaise. Add the bun top and serve.

Flounder Fillets

Prep time: 10 minutes | Cook time: 5 to 8 minutes | Serves 4

1 egg white
1 tablespoon water
1 cup panko bread crumbs
2 tablespoons extra-light virgin
olive oil

4 (4-ounce / 113-g) flounder
fillets
Salt and pepper, to taste
Oil for misting or cooking spray

1. Preheat the air fryer to 390ºF (199ºC). 2. Beat together egg white and water in shallow dish. 3. In another shallow dish, mix panko crumbs and oil until well combined and crumbly (best done by hand). 4. Season flounder fillets with salt and pepper to taste. Dip each fillet into egg mixture and then roll in panko crumbs, pressing in crumbs so that fish is nicely coated. 5. Spray the air fryer basket with nonstick cooking spray and add fillets. Air fry at 390ºF (199ºC) for 3 minutes. 6. Spray fish fillets but do not turn. Cook 2 to 5 minutes longer or until golden brown and crispy. Using a spatula, carefully remove fish from basket and serve.

Chili Prawns

Prep time: 10 minutes | Cook time: 8 minutes | Serves 2

8 prawns, cleaned
Salt and black pepper, to taste
½ teaspoon ground cayenne pepper
½ teaspoon garlic powder
½ teaspoon ground cumin
½ teaspoon red chili flakes
Cooking spray

1. Preheat the air fryer to 340ºF (171ºC). Spritz the air fryer basket with cooking spray. 2. Toss the remaining ingredients in a large bowl until the prawns are well coated. 3. Spread the coated prawns evenly in the basket and spray them with cooking spray. 4. Air fry for 8 minutes, flipping the prawns halfway through, or until the prawns are pink. 5. Remove the prawns from the basket to a plate.

Almond-Crusted Fish

Prep time: 15 minutes | Cook time: 10 minutes | Serves 4

4 (4-ounce / 113-g) fish fillets
¾ cup bread crumbs
¼ cup sliced almonds, crushed
2 tablespoons lemon juice
⅛ teaspoon cayenne
Salt and pepper, to taste
¾ cup flour
1 egg, beaten with 1 tablespoon water
Oil for misting or cooking spray

1. Split fish fillets lengthwise down the center to create 8 pieces. 2. Mix bread crumbs and almonds together and set aside. 3. Mix the lemon juice and cayenne together. Brush on all sides of fish. 4. Season fish to taste with salt and pepper. 5. Place the flour on a sheet of wax paper. 6. Roll fillets in flour, dip in egg wash, and roll in the crumb mixture. 7. Mist both sides of fish with oil or cooking spray. 8. Spray the air fryer basket and lay fillets inside. 9. Roast at 390ºF (199ºC) for 5 minutes, turn fish over, and cook for an additional 5 minutes or until fish is done and flakes easily.

Italian Tuna Roast

Prep time: 15 minutes | Cook time: 21 to 24 minutes | Serves 8

Cooking spray
1 tablespoon Italian seasoning
⅛ teaspoon ground black pepper
1 tablespoon extra-light olive
oil
1 teaspoon lemon juice
1 tuna loin (approximately 2 pounds / 907 g, 3 to 4 inches thick)

1. Spray baking dish with cooking spray and place in air fryer basket. Preheat the air fryer to 390ºF (199ºC). 2. Mix together the Italian seasoning, pepper, oil, and lemon juice. 3. Using a dull table knife or butter knife, pierce top of tuna about every half inch: Insert knife into top of tuna roast and pierce almost all the way to the bottom. 4. Spoon oil mixture into each of the holes and use the knife to push seasonings into the tuna as deeply as possible. 5. Spread any remaining oil mixture on all outer surfaces of tuna. 6. Place tuna roast in baking dish and roast at 390ºF (199ºC) for 20 minutes. Check temperature with a meat thermometer. Cook for an additional 1 to 4 minutes or until temperature reaches 145ºF (63ºC). 7. Remove basket from the air fryer and let tuna sit in the basket for 10 minutes.

Tuna Patty Sliders

Prep time: 15 minutes | Cook time: 10 to 15 minutes | Serves 4

3 (5-ounce / 142-g) cans tuna, packed in water
⅔ cup whole-wheat panko bread crumbs
⅓ cup shredded Parmesan
cheese
1 tablespoon sriracha
¾ teaspoon black pepper
10 whole-wheat slider buns
Cooking spray

Preheat the air fryer to 350ºF (177ºC). 2. Spray the air fryer basket lightly with cooking spray. 3. In a medium bowl combine the tuna, bread crumbs, Parmesan cheese, sriracha, and black pepper and stir to combine. 4. Form the mixture into 10 patties. 5. Place the patties in the air fryer basket in a single layer. Spray the patties lightly with cooking spray. You may need to cook them in batches. 6. Air fry for 6 to 8 minutes. Turn the patties over and lightly spray with cooking spray. Air fry until golden brown and crisp, another 4 to 7 more minutes. Serve warm.

Pecan-Crusted Catfish

Prep time: 5 minutes | Cook time: 12 minutes | Serves 4

½ cup pecan meal
1 teaspoon fine sea salt
¼ teaspoon ground black pepper
4 (4-ounce / 113-g) catfish
fillets
For Garnish (Optional):
Fresh oregano
Pecan halves

1. Spray the air fryer basket with avocado oil. Preheat the air fryer to 375ºF (191ºC). 2. In a large bowl, mix the pecan meal, salt, and pepper. One at a time, dredge the catfish fillets in the mixture, coating them well. Use your hands to press the pecan meal into the fillets. Spray the fish with avocado oil and place them in the air fryer basket. 3. Air fry the coated catfish for 12 minutes, or until it flakes easily and is no longer translucent in the center, flipping halfway through. 4. Garnish with oregano sprigs and pecan halves, if desired. 5. Store leftovers in an airtight container in the fridge for up to 3 days. Reheat in a preheated 350ºF (177ºC) air fryer for 4 minutes, or until heated through.

Rainbow Salmon Kebabs

Prep time: 10 minutes | Cook time: 8 minutes | Serves 2

6 ounces (170 g) boneless, skinless salmon, cut into 1-inch cubes
¼ medium red onion, peeled and cut into 1-inch pieces
½ medium yellow bell pepper, seeded and cut into 1-inch

pieces
½ medium zucchini, trimmed and cut into ½-inch slices
1 tablespoon olive oil
½ teaspoon salt
¼ teaspoon ground black pepper

1. Using one (6-inch) skewer, skewer 1 piece salmon, then 1 piece onion, 1 piece bell pepper, and finally 1 piece zucchini. Repeat this pattern with additional skewers to make four kebabs total. Drizzle with olive oil and sprinkle with salt and black pepper. 2. Place kebabs into ungreased air fryer basket. Adjust the temperature to 400ºF (204ºC) and air fry for 8 minutes, turning kebabs halfway through cooking. Salmon will easily flake and have an internal temperature of at least 145ºF (63ºC) when done; vegetables will be tender. Serve warm.

South Indian Fried Fish

Prep time: 20 minutes | Cook time: 8 minutes | Serves 4

2 tablespoons olive oil
2 tablespoons fresh lime or lemon juice
1 teaspoon minced fresh ginger
1 clove garlic, minced
1 teaspoon ground turmeric
½ teaspoon kosher salt

¼ to ½ teaspoon cayenne pepper
1 pound (454 g) tilapia fillets (2 to 3 fillets)
Olive oil spray
Lime or lemon wedges (optional)

1. In a large bowl, combine the oil, lime juice, ginger, garlic, turmeric, salt, and cayenne. Stir until well combined; set aside. 2. Cut each tilapia fillet into three or four equal-size pieces. Add the fish to the bowl and gently mix until all of the fish is coated in the marinade. Marinate for 10 to 15 minutes at room temperature. (Don't marinate any longer or the acid in the lime juice will "cook" the fish.) 3. Spray the air fryer basket with olive oil spray. Place the fish in the basket and spray the fish. Set the air fryer to 325ºF (163ºC) for 3 minutes to partially cook the fish. Set the air fryer to 400ºF (204ºC) for 5 minutes to finish cooking and crisp up the fish. (Thinner pieces of fish will cook faster so you may want to check at the 3-minute mark of the second cooking time and remove those that are cooked through, and then add them back toward the end of the second cooking time to crisp.) 4. Carefully remove the fish from the basket. Serve hot, with lemon wedges if desired.

Swordfish Skewers with Caponata

Prep time: 15 minutes | Cook time: 20 minutes | Serves 2

1 (10-ounce / 283-g) small Italian eggplant, cut into 1-inch pieces
6 ounces (170 g) cherry tomatoes
3 scallions, cut into 2 inches long
2 tablespoons extra-virgin olive oil, divided
Salt and pepper, to taste
12 ounces (340 g) skinless swordfish steaks, 1¼ inches

thick, cut into 1-inch pieces
2 teaspoons honey, divided
2 teaspoons ground coriander, divided
1 teaspoon grated lemon zest, divided
1 teaspoon juice
4 (6-inch) wooden skewers
1 garlic clove, minced
½ teaspoon ground cumin
1 tablespoon chopped fresh basil

1. Preheat the air fryer to 400ºF (204ºC). 2. Toss eggplant, tomatoes, and scallions with 1 tablespoon oil, ¼ teaspoon salt, and ⅛ teaspoon pepper in bowl; transfer to air fryer basket. Air fry until eggplant is softened and browned and tomatoes have begun to burst, about 14 minutes, tossing halfway through cooking. Transfer vegetables to cutting board and set aside to cool slightly. 3. Pat swordfish dry with paper towels. Combine 1 teaspoon oil, 1 teaspoon honey, 1 teaspoon coriander, ½ teaspoon lemon zest, ⅛ teaspoon salt, and pinch pepper in a clean bowl. Add swordfish and toss to coat. Thread swordfish onto skewers, leaving about ¼ inch between each piece (3 or 4 pieces per skewer). 4. Arrange skewers in air fryer basket, spaced evenly apart. (Skewers may overlap slightly.) Return basket to air fryer and air fry until swordfish is browned and registers 140ºF (60ºC), 6 to 8 minutes, flipping and rotating skewers halfway through cooking. 5. Meanwhile, combine remaining 2 teaspoons oil, remaining 1 teaspoon honey, remaining 1 teaspoon coriander, remaining ½ teaspoon lemon zest, lemon juice, garlic, cumin, ¼ teaspoon salt, and ⅛ teaspoon pepper in large bowl. Microwave, stirring once, until fragrant, about 30 seconds. Coarsely chop the cooked vegetables, transfer to bowl with dressing, along with any accumulated juices, and gently toss to combine. Stir in basil and season with salt and pepper to taste. Serve skewers with caponata.

Chapter 5 Desserts

Brownies for Two

Prep time: 5 minutes | Cook time: 15 minutes | Serves 2

½ cup blanched finely ground almond flour

3 tablespoons granular erythritol

3 tablespoons unsweetened cocoa powder

½ teaspoon baking powder

1 teaspoon vanilla extract

2 large eggs, whisked

2 tablespoons salted butter, melted

1 cup strawberries, for garnish

1. In a medium bowl, combine flour, erythritol, cocoa powder, and baking powder. 2. Add in vanilla, eggs, and butter, and stir until a thick batter forms. 3. Pour batter into a cake pan greased with cooking spray and place the pan into air fryer basket. Adjust the temperature to 325ºF (163ºC) and bake for 15 minutes. Centers will be firm when done. Let ramekins cool 5 minutes and top with strawberries before serving.

Mini Cheesecake

Prep time: 10 minutes | Cook time: 15 minutes | Serves 2

2 strawberries

2 tablespoons salted butter

2 tablespoons granular erythritol

4 ounces (113 g) full-fat cream

cheese, softened

1 large egg

½ teaspoon vanilla extract

⅛ cup powdered erythritol

1. Place butter, and granular erythritol in a food processor. Pulse until ingredients stick together and a dough forms. 2. Press dough into two ramekins then place the ramekins into the air fryer basket. 3. Adjust the temperature to 400ºF (204ºC) and bake for 5 minutes. 4. When done, remove the crust and let cool. 5. In a medium bowl, mix cream cheese with egg, vanilla extract, and powdered erythritol until smooth. 6. Spoon mixture on top of baked crust and place into the air fryer basket. 7. Adjust the temperature to 300ºF (149ºC) and bake for 10 minutes. 8. Once done, chill for 2 hours, transfer them into cake paper cups and top with strawberries before serving.

Chocolate and Rum Cupcakes

Prep time: 5 minutes | Cook time: 15 minutes | Serves 6

¾ cup granulated erythritol
1¼ cups almond flour
1 teaspoon unsweetened baking powder
3 teaspoons cocoa powder
½ teaspoon baking soda
½ teaspoon ground cinnamon
¼ teaspoon grated nutmeg
⅛ teaspoon salt

½ cup milk
1 stick butter, at room temperature
3 eggs, whisked
1 teaspoon pure rum extract
½ cup walnuts
¼ chocolate sauce, for drizzling
Cooking spray

1. Preheat the air fryer to 345ºF (174ºC). Spray a 6-cup muffin tin with cooking spray. 2. In a mixing bowl, combine the erythritol, almond flour, baking powder, cocoa powder, baking soda, cinnamon, nutmeg, and salt and stir until well blended. 3. In another mixing bowl, mix together the milk, butter, egg, and rum extract until thoroughly combined. Slowly and carefully pour this mixture into the bowl of dry mixture. 4. Spoon the batter into the greased muffin cups, filling each about three-quarters full. 5. Bake for 15 minutes, or until the center is springy and a toothpick inserted in the middle comes out clean. 6. Remove from the basket and place on a wire rack to cool. Top with walnuts and chocolate sauce and serve immediately.

Brown Sugar Banana Bread

Prep time: 20 minutes | Cook time: 22 to 24 minutes | Serves 4

1 cup packed light brown sugar
1 large egg, beaten
2 tablespoons butter, melted
½ cup milk, whole or 2%
2 cups all-purpose flour
1½ teaspoons baking powder

1 teaspoon ground cinnamon
½ teaspoon salt
1 banana, mashed
1 to 2 tablespoons oil
¼ cup confectioners' sugar (optional)

1. In a large bowl, stir together the brown sugar, egg, melted butter, and milk. 2. In a medium bowl, whisk the flour, baking powder, cinnamon, and salt until blended. Add the flour mixture to the sugar mixture and stir just to blend. 3. Add the mashed banana and stir to combine. 4. Preheat the air fryer to 350ºF (177ºC). Spritz 2 mini loaf pans with oil. 5. Evenly divide the batter between the prepared pans and place them in the air fryer basket. 6. Cook for 22 to 24 minutes, or until a knife inserted into the middle of the loaves comes out clean. 7. Dust the warm loaves with confectioners' sugar (if using).

Butter Flax Cookies

Prep time: 25 minutes | Cook time: 20 minutes | Serves 4

8 ounces (227 g) almond meal
2 tablespoons flaxseed meal
1 ounce (28 g) monk fruit
1 teaspoon baking powder
A pinch of grated nutmeg
A pinch of coarse salt
1 large egg, room temperature.
1 stick butter, room temperature
1 teaspoon vanilla extract

Mix the almond meal, flaxseed meal, monk fruit, baking powder, grated nutmeg, and salt in a bowl. 2. In a separate bowl, whisk the egg, butter, and vanilla extract. 3. Stir the egg mixture into dry mixture; mix to combine well or until it forms a nice, soft dough. 4. Roll your dough out and cut out with a cookie cutter of your choice. Bake in the preheated air fryer at 350ºF (177ºC) for 10 minutes. Decrease the temperature to 330ºF (166ºC) and cook for 10 minutes longer. Bon appétit!

Vanilla Scones

Prep time: 20 minutes | Cook time: 10 minutes | Serves 6

4 ounces (113 g) coconut flour
½ teaspoon baking powder
1 teaspoon apple cider vinegar
2 teaspoons mascarpone
¼ cup heavy cream
1 teaspoon vanilla extract
1 tablespoon erythritol
Cooking spray

1. In the mixing bowl, mix coconut flour with baking powder, apple cider vinegar, mascarpone, heavy cream, vanilla extract, and erythritol. 2. Knead the dough and cut into scones. 3. Then put them in the air fryer basket and sprinkle with cooking spray. 4. Cook the vanilla scones at 365ºF (185ºC) for 10 minutes.

Pretzels

Prep time: 10 minutes | Cook time: 10 minutes | Serves 6

1½ cups shredded Mozzarella cheese
1 cup blanched finely ground almond flour
2 tablespoons salted butter,
melted, divided
¼ cup granular erythritol, divided
1 teaspoon ground cinnamon

1. Place Mozzarella, flour, 1 tablespoon butter, and 2 tablespoons erythritol in a large microwave-safe bowl. Microwave on high 45 seconds, then stir with a fork until a smooth dough ball forms. 2. Separate dough into six equal sections. Gently roll each section into a 12-inch rope, then fold into a pretzel shape. 3. Place pretzels into ungreased air fryer basket. Adjust the temperature to 370ºF (188ºC) and set the timer for 8 minutes, turning pretzels halfway through cooking. 4. In a small bowl, combine remaining butter, remaining erythritol, and cinnamon. Brush ½ mixture on both sides of pretzels. 5. Place pretzels back into air fryer and cook an additional 2 minutes at 370ºF (188ºC). 6. Transfer pretzels to a large plate. Brush on both sides with remaining butter mixture, then let cool 5 minutes before serving.

Easy Chocolate Donuts

Prep time: 5 minutes | Cook time: 8 minutes | Serves 8

1 (8-ounce / 227-g) can jumbo biscuits
Cooking oil
½ cup nuts
Chocolate sauce, for drizzling

1. Preheat the air fryer to 375ºF (191ºC) 2. Separate the biscuit dough into 8 biscuits and place them on a flat work surface. Use a small circle cookie cutter or a biscuit cutter to cut a hole in the center of each biscuit. You can also cut the holes using a knife. 3. Spray the air fryer basket with cooking oil. 4. Put 4 donuts in the air fryer. Do not stack. Spray with cooking oil. Air fry for 4 minutes. 5. Open the air fryer and flip the donuts. Air fry for an additional 4 minutes. 6. Remove the cooked donuts from the air fryer, then repeat steps 3 and 4 for the remaining 4 donuts. 7. Drizzle chocolate sauce over the donuts and sprinkle with crushed nuts before serving warm.

Cinnamon Cupcakes with Cream Cheese Frosting

Prep time: 10 minutes | Cook time: 20 to 25 minutes | Serves 6

½ cup plus 2 tablespoons almond flour

2 tablespoons low-carb vanilla protein powder

⅛ teaspoon salt

1 teaspoon baking powder

¼ teaspoon ground cinnamon

¼ cup unsalted butter

¼ cup Swerve

1 tablespoon crushed peanuts

2 eggs

½ teaspoon vanilla extract

2 tablespoons heavy cream

Cream Cheese Frosting:

4 ounces (113 g) cream cheese, softened

2 tablespoons unsalted butter, softened

½ teaspoon vanilla extract

2 tablespoons powdered Swerve

1 to 2 tablespoons heavy cream

1. Preheat the air fryer to 320ºF (160ºC). Lightly coat 6 silicone muffin cups with oil and set aside. 2. In a medium bowl, combine the almond flour, protein powder, salt, baking powder, and cinnamon; set aside. 3. In a stand mixer fitted with a paddle attachment, beat the butter and Swerve until creamy. Add the eggs, vanilla, and heavy cream, and beat again until thoroughly combined. Add half the flour mixture at a time to the butter mixture, mixing after each addition, until you have a smooth, creamy batter. 4. Divide the batter evenly among the muffin cups, filling each one about three-fourths full. Arrange the muffin cups in the air fryer and air fry for 20 to 25 minutes, or until a toothpick inserted into the center of a cupcake comes out clean. Transfer the cupcakes to a rack and let cool completely. 5. To make the cream cheese frosting: In a stand mixer fitted with a paddle attachment, beat the cream cheese, butter, and vanilla until fluffy. Add the Swerve and mix again until thoroughly combined. With the mixer running, add the heavy cream a tablespoon at a time until the frosting is smooth and creamy. Frost the cupcakes as desired and sprinkle the peanuts.

Coconut Macaroons

Prep time: 5 minutes | Cook time: 8 to 10 minutes | Makes 12 macaroons

1⅓ cups shredded, sweetened coconut

4½ teaspoons flour

2 tablespoons sugar

1 egg white

½ teaspoon almond extract

1. Preheat the air fryer to 330ºF (166ºC). 2. Mix all ingredients together. 3. Shape coconut mixture into 12 balls. 4. Place all 12 macaroons in air fryer basket. They won't expand, so you can place them close together, but they shouldn't touch. 5. Air fry at 330ºF (166ºC) for 8 to 10 minutes, until golden.

Chocolate Croissants

Prep time: 5 minutes | Cook time: 24 minutes | Serves 8

1 sheet frozen puff pastry, thawed

⅓ cup chocolate-hazelnut

spread

1 large egg, beaten

On a lightly floured surface, roll puff pastry into a 14-inch square. Cut pastry into quarters to form 4 squares. Cut each square diagonally to form 8 triangles. 2. Spread 2 teaspoons chocolate-hazelnut spread on each triangle; from wider end, roll up pastry. Brush egg on top of each roll. 3. Preheat the air fryer to 375°F (191°C). Air fry rolls in batches, 3 or 4 at a time, 8 minutes per batch, or until pastry is golden brown. 4. Cool on a wire rack; serve while warm or at room temperature.

Indian Toast and Milk

Prep time: 10 minutes | Cook time: 20 minutes | Serves 4

1 cup sweetened condensed milk

1 cup evaporated milk

1 cup half-and-half

1 cup strawberries

1 cup blueberries

1 teaspoon ground cardamom,

plus additional for garnish

4 slices white bread

2 to 3 tablespoons ghee or butter, softened

2 tablespoons crushed pistachios, for garnish (optional)

1. In a baking pan, combine the condensed milk, evaporated milk, half-and-half, and cardamom. Stir until well combined. 2. Place the pan in the air fryer basket. Set the air fryer to 350°F (177°C) for 15 minutes, stirring halfway through the cooking time. Remove the sweetened milk from the air fryer and set aside. 3. Brush each side of bread with ghee. Place the bread in the air fryer basket. Set the air fryer to 350°F (177°C) for 5 minutes or until golden brown and toasty. 4. Remove the bread from the air fryer. Arrange 1 bread slice in each of four wide, shallow bowls. Pour the hot milk mixture on top of the bread and let soak for 30 minutes. 5. Garnish with strawberries and blueberries if using, and sprinkle with additional cardamom.

Almond Shortbread

Prep time: 10 minutes | Cook time: 12 minutes | Serves 8

½ cup (1 stick) unsalted butter

½ cup sugar

1 teaspoon pure almond extract

1 cup all-purpose flour

1. In bowl of a stand mixer fitted with the paddle attachment, beat the butter and sugar on medium speed until light and fluffy, 3 to 4 minutes. Add the almond extract and beat until combined, about 30 seconds. Turn the mixer to low. Add the flour a little at a time and beat for about 2 minutes more until well-incorporated. 2. Pat the dough into an even layer in a baking pan. Place the pan in the air fryer basket. Set the air fryer to 375ºF (191ºC) for 12 minutes. 3. Carefully remove the pan from air fryer basket. While the shortbread is still warm and soft, cut it into 8 wedges. 4. Let cool in the pan on a wire rack for 5 minutes. Remove the wedges from the pan and let cool completely on the rack before serving.

Olive Oil Cake

Prep time: 10 minutes | Cook time: 30 minutes | Serves 8

2 cups blanched finely ground almond flour

5 large eggs, whisked

¾ cup extra-virgin olive oil

⅓ cup granular erythritol

1 teaspoon vanilla extract

1 teaspoon baking powder

1. In a large bowl, mix all ingredients. Pour batter into an ungreased round nonstick baking dish. 2. Place dish into air fryer basket. Adjust the temperature to 300ºF (149ºC) and bake for 30 minutes. The cake will be golden on top and firm in the center when done. 3. Let cake cool in dish 30 minutes before slicing and serving.

Lush Chocolate Chip Cookies

Prep time: 7 minutes | Cook time: 9 minutes | Serves 4

3 tablespoons butter, at room temperature
⅓ cup plus 1 tablespoon light brown sugar
1 egg yolk
½ cup all-purpose flour
2 tablespoons ground white

chocolate
¼ teaspoon baking soda
½ teaspoon vanilla extract
¾ cup semisweet chocolate chips
Nonstick flour-infused baking spray

In medium bowl, beat together the butter and brown sugar until fluffy. Stir in the egg yolk. 2. Add the flour, white chocolate, baking soda, and vanilla and mix well. Stir in the chocolate chips. 3. Line a 6-by-2-inch round baking pan with parchment paper. Spray the parchment paper with flour-infused baking spray. 4. Insert the crisper plate into the basket and the basket into the unit. Preheat the unit by selecting BAKE, setting the temperature to 300ºF (149ºC), and setting the time to 3 minutes. Select START/STOP to begin. 5. Spread the batter into the prepared pan, leaving a ½-inch border on all sides. 6. Once the unit is preheated, place the pan into the basket. 7. Select BAKE, set the temperature to 300ºF (149ºC), and set the time to 9 minutes. Select START/STOP to begin. 8. When the cooking is complete, the cookie should be light brown and just barely set. Remove the pan from the basket and let cool for 10 minutes. Remove the cookie from the pan, remove the parchment paper, and let cool completely on a wire rack.

Gingerbread

Prep time: 5 minutes | Cook time: 20 minutes |
Makes 1 loaf

Cooking spray
1 cup flour
2 tablespoons sugar
¾ teaspoon ground ginger
¼ teaspoon cinnamon
1 teaspoon baking powder
½ teaspoon baking soda

⅛ teaspoon salt
1 egg
¼ cup molasses
½ cup buttermilk
2 tablespoons oil
1 teaspoon pure vanilla extract

Preheat the air fryer to 330ºF (166ºC). 2. Spray a baking dish lightly with cooking spray. 3. In a medium bowl, mix together all the dry ingredients. 4. In a separate bowl, beat the egg. Add molasses, buttermilk, oil, and vanilla and stir until well mixed. 5. Pour liquid mixture into dry ingredients and stir until well blended. 6. Pour batter into baking dish and bake at 330ºF (166ºC) for 20 minutes or until toothpick inserted in center of loaf comes out clean.

Crispy Pineapple Rings

Prep time: 5 minutes | Cook time: 6 to 8 minutes | Serves 6

1 cup rice milk
⅔ cup flour
½ cup water
¼ cup unsweetened flaked coconut
4 tablespoons sugar
½ teaspoon baking soda

½ teaspoon baking powder
½ teaspoon vanilla essence
½ teaspoon ground cinnamon
¼ teaspoon ground anise star
Pinch of kosher salt
1 medium pineapple, peeled and sliced

Preheat the air fryer to 380ºF (193ºC). 2. In a large bowl, stir together all the ingredients except the pineapple. 3. Dip each pineapple slice into the batter until evenly coated. 4. Arrange the pineapple slices in the basket and air fry for 6 to 8 minutes until golden brown. 5. Remove from the basket to a plate and cool for 5 minutes before serving.arm.

Cream Cheese Danish

Prep time: 20 minutes | Cook time: 15 minutes | Serves 6

¾ cup blanched finely ground almond flour
1 cup shredded Mozzarella cheese
5 ounces (142 g) full-fat cream cheese, divided

2 large egg yolks
¾ cup powdered erythritol, divided
2 teaspoons vanilla extract, divided

1. In a large microwave-safe bowl, add almond flour, Mozzarella, and 1 ounce (28 g) cream cheese. Mix and then microwave for 1 minute. 2. Stir and add egg yolks to the bowl. Continue stirring until soft dough forms. Add ½ cup erythritol to dough and 1 teaspoon vanilla. 3. Cut a piece of parchment to fit your air fryer basket. Wet your hands with warm water and press out the dough into a ¼-inch-thick rectangle. 4. In a medium bowl, mix remaining cream cheese, erythritol, and vanilla. Place this cream cheese mixture on the right half of the dough rectangle. Fold over the left side of the dough and press to seal. Place into the air fryer basket. 5. Adjust the temperature to 330ºF (166ºC) and bake for 15 minutes. 6. After 7 minutes, flip over the Danish. 7. When done, remove the Danish from parchment and allow to completely cool before cutting.

Blackberry Peach Cobbler with Vanilla

Prep time: 10 minutes | Cook time: 20 minutes | Serves 4

Filling:
1 (6-ounce / 170-g) package blackberries
1½ cups chopped peaches, cut into ½-inch thick slices
2 teaspoons arrowroot or cornstarch
2 tablespoons coconut sugar
1 teaspoon lemon juice
Topping:

2 tablespoons sunflower oil
1 tablespoon maple syrup
1 teaspoon vanilla
3 tablespoons coconut sugar
½ cup rolled oats
⅓ cup whole-wheat pastry flour
1 teaspoon cinnamon
¼ teaspoon nutmeg
⅛ teaspoon sea salt

Make the Filling: 1. Combine the blackberries, peaches, arrowroot, coconut sugar, and lemon juice in a baking pan. 2. Using a rubber spatula, stir until well incorporated. Set aside. Make the Topping: 3. Preheat the air fryer to 320ºF (160ºC) 4. Combine the oil, maple syrup, and vanilla in a mixing bowl and stir well. Whisk in the remaining ingredients. Spread this mixture evenly over the filling. 5. Place the pan in the air fryer basket and bake for 20 minutes, or until the topping is crispy and golden brown. Serve warm

Peaches and Apple Crumble

Prep time: 10 minutes | Cook time: 10 to 12 minutes | Serves 4

2 peaches, peeled, pitted, and chopped
1 apple, peeled and chopped
2 tablespoons honey
½ cup quick-cooking oatmeal
⅓ cup whole-wheat pastry flour
2 tablespoons unsalted butter, at room temperature
3 tablespoons packed brown sugar
½ teaspoon ground cinnamon

Preheat the air fryer to 380ºF (193ºC). 2. Mix together the peaches, apple, and honey in a baking pan until well incorporated. 3. In a bowl, combine the oatmeal, pastry flour, butter, brown sugar, and cinnamon and stir to mix well. Spread this mixture evenly over the fruit. 4. Place the baking pan in the air fryer basket and bake for 10 to 12 minutes, or until the fruit is bubbling around the edges and the topping is golden brown. 5. Remove from the basket and serve warm.

Glazed Cherry Turnovers

Prep time: 10 minutes | Cook time: 14 minutes per batch | Serves 8

2 sheets frozen puff pastry, thawed
1 (21-ounce / 595-g) can premium cherry pie filling
2 teaspoons ground cinnamon
1 egg, beaten
1 cup sliced almonds
1 cup powdered sugar
2 tablespoons milk

Roll a sheet of puff pastry out into a square that is approximately 10-inches by 10-inches. Cut this large square into quarters. 2. Mix the cherry pie filling and cinnamon together in a bowl. Spoon ¼ cup of the cherry filling into the center of each puff pastry square. Brush the perimeter of the pastry square with the egg wash. Fold one corner of the puff pastry over the cherry pie filling towards the opposite corner, forming a triangle. Seal the two edges of the pastry together with the tip of a fork, making a design with the tines. Brush the top of the turnovers with the egg wash and sprinkle sliced almonds over each one. Repeat these steps with the second sheet of puff pastry. You should have eight turnovers at the end. 3. Preheat the air fryer to 370ºF (188ºC). 4. Air fry two turnovers at a time for 14 minutes, carefully turning them over halfway through the cooking time. 5. While the turnovers are cooking, make the glaze by whisking the powdered sugar and milk together in a small bowl until smooth. Let the glaze sit for a minute so the sugar can absorb the milk. If the consistency is still too thick to drizzle, add a little more milk, a drop at a time, and stir until smooth. 6. Let the cooked cherry turnovers sit for at least 10 minutes. Then drizzle the glaze over each turnover in a zigzag motion. Serve warm or at room temperature.

Pumpkin Spice Pecans

Prep time: 5 minutes | Cook time: 6 minutes | Serves 4

1 cup whole pecans
¼ cup granular erythritol
1 large egg white
½ teaspoon ground cinnamon
½ teaspoon pumpkin pie spice
½ teaspoon vanilla extract

1. Toss all ingredients in a large bowl until pecans are coated. Place into the air fryer basket. 2. Adjust the temperature to 300ºF (149ºC) and air fry for 6 minutes. 3. Toss two to three times during cooking. 4. Allow to cool completely. Store in an airtight container up to 3 days.

Cinnamon and Pecan Pie

Prep time: 10 minutes | Cook time: 25 minutes | Serves 4

1 pie dough
½ teaspoons cinnamon
¾ teaspoon vanilla extract
2 eggs
¾ cup maple syrup
⅛ teaspoon nutmeg
3 tablespoons melted butter, divided
2 tablespoons sugar
½ cup chopped pecans

1. Preheat the air fryer to 370ºF (188ºC). 2. In a small bowl, coat the pecans in 1 tablespoon of melted butter. 3. Transfer the pecans to the air fryer and air fry for about 10 minutes. 4. Put the pie dough in a greased pie pan and add the pecans on top. 5. In a bowl, mix the rest of the ingredients. Pour this over the pecans. 6. Put the pan in the air fryer and bake for 25 minutes. 7. Serve immediately.

Lemon Raspberry Muffins

Prep time: 5 minutes | Cook time: 15 minutes | Serves 6

2 cups almond flour
¾ cup Swerve
1¼ teaspoons baking powder
⅓ teaspoon ground allspice
⅓ teaspoon ground anise star
½ teaspoon grated lemon zest
¼ teaspoon salt
2 eggs
1 cup sour cream
½ cup coconut oil
½ cup raspberries

Preheat the air fryer to 345ºF (174ºC). Line a muffin pan with 6 paper liners. 2. In a mixing bowl, mix the almond flour, Swerve, baking powder, allspice, anise, lemon zest, and salt. 3. In another mixing bowl, beat the eggs, sour cream, and coconut oil until well mixed. Add the egg mixture to the flour mixture and stir to combine. Mix in the raspberries. 4. Scrape the batter into the prepared muffin cups, filling each about three-quarters full. 5. Bake for 15 minutes, or until the tops are golden and a toothpick inserted in the middle comes out clean. 6. Allow the muffins to cool for 10 minutes in the muffin pan before removing and serving.

Berry Crumble

Prep time: 10 minutes | Cook time: 15 minutes | Serves 4

For the Filling:
2 cups mixed berries
2 tablespoons sugar
1 tablespoon cornstarch
1 tablespoon fresh lemon juice
For the Topping:
¼ cup all-purpose flour

¼ cup rolled oats
1 tablespoon sugar
2 tablespoons cold unsalted butter, cut into small cubes
Whipped cream or ice cream (optional)

1. Preheat the air fryer to 400ºF (204ºC). 2. For the filling: In a round baking pan, gently mix the berries, sugar, cornstarch, and lemon juice until thoroughly combined. 3. For the topping: In a small bowl, combine the flour, oats, and sugar. Stir the butter into the flour mixture until the mixture has the consistency of bread crumbs. 4. Sprinkle the topping over the berries. 5. Put the pan in the air fryer basket and air fry for 15 minutes. Let cool for 5 minutes on a wire rack. 6. Serve topped with whipped cream or ice cream, if desired.

Strawberry Pastry Rolls

Prep time: 20 minutes | Cook time: 5 to 6 minutes per batch | Serves 4

3 ounces (85 g) low-fat cream cheese
2 tablespoons plain yogurt
2 teaspoons sugar
¼ teaspoon pure vanilla extract
8 ounces (227 g) fresh

strawberries
8 sheets phyllo dough
Butter-flavored cooking spray
¼ to ½ cup dark chocolate chips (optional)

1. In a medium bowl, combine the cream cheese, yogurt, sugar, and vanilla. Beat with hand mixer at high speed until smooth, about 1 minute. 2. Wash strawberries and destem. Chop enough of them to measure ½ cup. Stir into cheese mixture. 3. Preheat the air fryer to 330ºF (166ºC). 4. Phyllo dough dries out quickly, so cover your stack of phyllo sheets with waxed paper and then place a damp dish towel on top of that. Remove only one sheet at a time as you work. 5. To create one pastry roll, lay out a single sheet of phyllo. Spray lightly with butter-flavored spray, top with a second sheet of phyllo, and spray the second sheet lightly. 6. Place a quarter of the filling (about 3 tablespoons) about ½ inch from the edge of one short side. Fold the end of the phyllo over the filling and keep rolling a turn or two. Fold in both the left and right sides so that the edges meet in the middle of your roll. Then roll up completely. Spray outside of pastry roll with butter spray. 7. When you have 4 rolls, place them in the air fryer basket, seam side down, leaving some space in between each. Air fry at 330ºF (166ºC) for 5 to 6 minutes, until they turn a delicate golden brown. 8. Repeat step 7 for remaining

rolls. 9. Allow pastries to cool to room temperature. 10. When ready to serve, slice the remaining strawberries. If desired, melt the chocolate chips in microwave or double boiler. Place 1 pastry on each dessert plate, and top with sliced strawberries. Drizzle melted chocolate over strawberries and onto plate.

Pears with Honey-Lemon Ricotta

Prep time: 10 minutes | Cook time: 8 minutes | Serves 4

2 large Bartlett pears
3 tablespoons butter, melted
3 tablespoons brown sugar
½ teaspoon ground ginger
¼ teaspoon ground cardamom
½ cup whole-milk ricotta

cheese
1 tablespoon honey, plus additional for drizzling
1 teaspoon pure almond extract
1 teaspoon pure lemon extract

1. Peel each pear and cut in half lengthwise. Use a melon baller to scoop out the core. Place the pear halves in a medium bowl, add the melted butter, and toss. Add the brown sugar, ginger, and cardamom; toss to coat. 2. Place the pear halves, cut side down, in the air fryer basket. Set the air fryer to 375ºF (191ºC) for 8 to 10 minutes, or until the pears are lightly browned and tender, but not mushy. 3. Meanwhile, in a medium bowl, combine the ricotta, honey, and almond and lemon extracts. Beat with an electric mixer on medium speed until the mixture is light and fluffy, about 1 minute. 4. To serve, divide the ricotta mixture among four small shallow bowls. Place a pear half, cut side up, on top of the cheese. Drizzle with additional honey and serve.

Cream Cheese Shortbread Cookies

Prep time: 30 minutes | Cook time: 20 minutes | Makes 12 cookies

¼ cup coconut oil, melted
2 ounces (57 g) cream cheese, softened
½ cup granular erythritol

1 large egg, whisked
2 cups blanched finely ground almond flour
1 teaspoon almond extract

1. Combine all ingredients in a large bowl to form a firm ball. 2. Place dough on a sheet of plastic wrap and roll into a 12-inch-long log shape. Roll log in plastic wrap and place in refrigerator 30 minutes to chill. 3. Remove log from plastic and slice into twelve equal cookies. Cut two sheets of parchment paper to fit air fryer basket. Place six cookies on each ungreased sheet. Place one sheet with cookies into air fryer basket. Adjust the temperature to 320ºF (160ºC) and bake for 10 minutes, turning cookies halfway through cooking. They will be lightly golden when done. Repeat with remaining cookies. 4. Let cool 15 minutes before serving to avoid crumbling.

Tortilla Fried Pies

Prep time: 10 minutes | Cook time: 5 minutes per batch | Makes 12 pies

12 small flour tortillas (4-inch diameter)	2 tablespoons shredded, unsweetened coconut
½ cup fig preserves	Oil for misting or cooking spray
¼ cup sliced almonds	

1. Wrap refrigerated tortillas in damp paper towels and heat in microwave 30 seconds to warm. 2. Working with one tortilla at a time, place 2 teaspoons fig preserves, 1 teaspoon sliced almonds, and ½ teaspoon coconut in the center of each. 3. Moisten outer edges of tortilla all around. 4. Fold one side of tortilla over filling to make a half-moon shape and press down lightly on center. Using the tines of a fork, press down firmly on edges of tortilla to seal in filling. 5. Mist both sides with oil or cooking spray. 6. Place hand pies in air fryer basket close but not overlapping. It's fine to lean some against the sides and corners of the basket. You may need to cook in 2 batches. 7. Air fry at 390ºF (199ºC) for 5 minutes or until lightly browned. Serve hot. 8. Refrigerate any leftover pies in a closed container. To serve later, toss them back in the air fryer basket and cook for 2 or 3 minutes to reheat.

Lemon Poppy Seed Macaroons

Prep time: 10 minutes | Cook time: 14 minutes | Makes 1 dozen cookies

2 large egg whites, room temperature	1 teaspoon lemon extract
⅓ cup Swerve confectioners'-style sweetener or equivalent amount of powdered sweetener	¼ teaspoon fine sea salt
	2 cups unsweetened shredded coconut
2 tablespoons grated lemon zest, plus more for garnish if desired	Lemon Icing:
	¼ cup Swerve confectioners'-style sweetener or equivalent amount of powdered sweetener
2 teaspoons poppy seeds	1 tablespoon lemon juice

1. Preheat the air fryer to 325ºF (163ºC). Line a pie pan or a casserole dish that will fit inside your air fryer with parchment paper. 2. Place the egg whites in a medium-sized bowl and use a hand mixer on high to beat the whites until stiff peaks form. Add the sweetener, lemon zest, poppy seeds, lemon extract, and salt. Mix on low until combined. Gently fold in the coconut with a rubber spatula. 3. Use a 1-inch cookie scoop to place the cookies on the parchment, spacing them about ¼ inch apart. Place the pan in the air fryer and bake for 12 to 14 minutes, until the cookies are golden and a toothpick inserted into the center comes out clean. 4. While the cookies bake, make the lemon icing: Place the sweetener in a small bowl. Add the lemon juice and stir well. If the icing is

too thin, add a little more sweetener. If the icing is too thick, add a little more lemon juice. 5. Remove the cookies from the air fryer and allow to cool for about 10 minutes, then drizzle with the icing. Garnish with lemon zest, if desired. Store leftovers in an airtight container in the fridge for up to 5 days or in the freezer for up to a month.

Applesauce and Chocolate Brownies

Prep time: 10 minutes | Cook time: 15 minutes | Serves 8

¼ cup unsweetened cocoa powder	½ cup granulated sugar
¼ cup all-purpose flour	1 large egg
¼ teaspoon kosher salt	3 tablespoons unsweetened applesauce
½ teaspoons baking powder	¼ cup miniature semisweet chocolate chips
3 tablespoons unsalted butter, melted	Coarse sea salt, to taste

Preheat the air fryer to 300ºF (149ºC). 2. In a large bowl, whisk together the cocoa powder, all-purpose flour, kosher salt, and baking powder. 3. In a separate large bowl, combine the butter, granulated sugar, egg, and applesauce, then use a spatula to fold in the cocoa powder mixture and the chocolate chips until well combined. 4. Spray a baking pan with nonstick cooking spray, then pour the mixture into the pan. Place the pan in the air fryer and bake for 15 minutes or until a toothpick comes out clean when inserted in the middle. 5. Remove the brownies from the air fryer, sprinkle some coarse sea salt on top, and allow to cool in the pan on a wire rack for 20 minutes before cutting and serving.

Baked Apples and Walnuts

Prep time: 6 minutes | Cook time: 20 minutes | Serves 4

4 small Granny Smith apples	1 teaspoon ground cinnamon
⅓ cup chopped walnuts	½ teaspoon ground nutmeg
¼ cup light brown sugar	½ cup water, or apple juice
2 tablespoons butter, melted	

Cut off the top third of the apples. Spoon out the core and some of the flesh and discard. Place the apples in a small air fryer baking pan. 2. Insert the crisper plate into the basket and the basket into the unit. Preheat the unit by selecting BAKE, setting the temperature to 350ºF (177ºC), and setting the time to 3 minutes. Select START/STOP to begin. 3. In a small bowl, stir together the walnuts, brown sugar, melted butter, cinnamon, and nutmeg. Spoon this mixture into the centers of the hollowed-out apples. 4. Once the unit is preheated, pour the water into the crisper plate. Place the baking pan into the basket. 5. Select BAKE, set the temperature to 350ºF (177ºC), and set the time to 20 minutes. Select START/STOP to begin. 6. When the cooking is complete, the apples should be bubbly and fork-tender.

Vanilla Cookies with Hazelnuts

Prep time: 20 minutes | Cook time: 10 minutes | Serves 6

1 cup almond flour	1 cup Swerve
½ cup coconut flour	2 teaspoons vanilla
1 teaspoon baking soda	2 eggs, at room temperature
1 teaspoon fine sea salt	1 cup hazelnuts, coarsely
1 stick butter	chopped

1. Preheat the air fryer to 350°F (177°C). 2. Mix the flour with the baking soda, and sea salt. 3. In the bowl of an electric mixer, beat the butter, Swerve, and vanilla until creamy. Fold in the eggs, one at a time, and mix until well combined. 4. Slowly and gradually, stir in the flour mixture. Finally, fold in the coarsely chopped hazelnuts. 5. Divide the dough into small balls using a large cookie scoop; drop onto the prepared cookie sheets. Bake for 10 minutes or until golden brown, rotating the pan once or twice through the cooking time. 6. Work in batches and cool for a couple of minutes before removing to wire racks. Enjoy!

Cherry Pie

Prep time: 15 minutes | Cook time: 35 minutes | Serves 6

All-purpose flour, for dusting	cherry pie filling
2 refrigerated piecrusts, at room	1 egg
temperature	1 tablespoon water
1 (12.5-ounce / 354-g) can	1 tablespoon sugar

1. Dust a work surface with flour and place the piecrust on it. Roll out the piecrust. Invert a shallow air fryer baking pan, or your own pie pan that fits inside the air fryer basket, on top of the dough. Trim the dough around the pan, making your cut ½ inch wider than the pan itself. 2. Repeat with the second piecrust but make the cut the same size as or slightly smaller than the pan. 3. Put the larger crust in the bottom of the baking pan. Don't stretch the dough. Gently press it into the pan. 4. Spoon in enough cherry pie filling to fill the crust. Do not overfill. 5. Using a knife or pizza cutter, cut the second piecrust into 1-inch-wide strips. Weave the strips in a lattice pattern over the top of the cherry pie filling. 6. Insert the crisper plate into the basket and the basket into the unit. Preheat the unit by selecting BAKE, setting the temperature to 325°F (163°C), and setting the time to 3 minutes. Select START/STOP to begin. 7. In a small bowl, whisk the egg and water. Gently brush the egg wash over the top of the pie. Sprinkle with the sugar and cover the pie with aluminum foil. 8. Once the unit is preheated, place the pie into the basket. 9. Select BAKE, set the temperature to 325°F (163°C), and set the time to 35 minutes. Select START/STOP to begin. 10. After 30 minutes, remove the foil and resume cooking for 3 to 5 minutes more. The finished pie should have a flaky golden brown crust and bubbling pie filling. 11. When the cooking is complete, serve warm. Refrigerate leftovers for a few days.

Double Chocolate Brownies

Prep time: 5 minutes | Cook time: 15 to 20 minutes | Serves 8

1 cup almond flour	½ cup unsalted butter, melted
½ cup unsweetened cocoa	and cooled
powder	3 eggs
½ teaspoon baking powder	1 teaspoon vanilla extract
⅓ cup Swerve	2 tablespoons mini semisweet
¼ teaspoon salt	chocolate chips

1. Preheat the air fryer to 350°F (177°C). Line a cake pan with parchment paper and brush with oil. 2. In a large bowl, combine the almond flour, cocoa powder, baking powder, Swerve, and salt. Add the butter, eggs, and vanilla. Stir until thoroughly combined. (The batter will be thick.) Spread the batter into the prepared pan and scatter the chocolate chips on top. 3. Air fry for 15 to 20 minutes until the edges are set. (The center should still appear slightly undercooked.) Let cool completely before slicing. To store, cover and refrigerate the brownies for up to 3 days.

Air Fryer Apple Fritters

Prep time: 30 minutes | Cook time: 7 to 8 minutes | Serves 6

1 cup chopped, peeled Granny	2 tablespoons milk
Smith apple	2 tablespoons butter, melted
½ cup granulated sugar	1 large egg, beaten
1 teaspoon ground cinnamon	Cooking spray
1 cup all-purpose flour	¼ cup confectioners' sugar
1 teaspoon baking powder	(optional)
1 teaspoon salt	

1. Mix together the apple, granulated sugar, and cinnamon in a small bowl. Allow to sit for 30 minutes. 2. Combine the flour, baking powder, and salt in a medium bowl. Add the milk, butter, and egg and stir to incorporate. 3. Pour the apple mixture into the bowl of flour mixture and stir with a spatula until a dough forms. 4. Make the fritters: On a clean work surface, divide the dough into 12 equal portions and shape into 1-inch balls. Flatten them into patties with your hands. 5. Preheat the air fryer to 350°F (177°C). Line the air fryer basket with parchment paper and spray it with cooking spray. 6. Transfer the apple fritters onto the parchment paper, evenly spaced but not too close together. Spray the fritters with cooking spray. 7. Bake for 7 to 8 minutes until lightly browned. Flip the fritters halfway through the cooking time. 8. Remove from the basket to a plate and serve with the confectioners' sugar sprinkled on top, if desired.

Lemon Bars

Prep time: 15 minutes | Cook time: 25 minutes | Serves 6

¾ cup whole-wheat pastry flour

2 tablespoons confectioners' sugar

¼ cup butter, melted

½ cup granulated sugar

1 tablespoon packed grated lemon zest

¼ cup freshly squeezed lemon juice

⅛ teaspoon sea salt

¼ cup unsweetened plain applesauce

2 teaspoons cornstarch

¾ teaspoon baking powder

Cooking oil spray (sunflower, safflower, or refined coconut)

1. In a small bowl, stir together the flour, confectioners' sugar, and melted butter just until well combined. Place in the refrigerator. 2. In a medium bowl, stir together the granulated sugar, lemon zest and juice, salt, applesauce, cornstarch, and baking powder. 3. Insert the crisper plate into the basket and the basket into the unit. Preheat the unit by selecting BAKE, setting the temperature to 350°F (177°C), and setting the time to 3 minutes. Select START/STOP to begin. 4. Spray a 6-by-2-inch round pan lightly with cooking oil. Remove the crust mixture from the refrigerator and gently press it into the bottom of the prepared pan in an even layer. 5. Once the unit is preheated, place the pan into the basket. 6. Select BAKE, set the temperature to 350°F (177°C), and set the time to 25 minutes. Select START/STOP to begin. 7. After 5 minutes, check the crust. It should be slightly firm to the touch. Remove the pan and spread the lemon filling over the crust. Reinsert the pan into the basket and resume baking for 18 to 20 minutes, or until the top is nicely browned. 8. When baking is complete, let cool for 30 minutes. Refrigerate to cool completely. Cut into pieces and serve.

Luscious Coconut Pie

Prep time: 5 minutes | Cook time: 45 minutes | Serves 6

1 cup plus ¼ cup unsweetened shredded coconut, divided

2 eggs

1½ cups almond milk

½ cup granulated Swerve

½ cup coconut flour

¼ cup unsalted butter, melted

1½ teaspoons vanilla extract

¼ teaspoon salt

2 tablespoons powdered Swerve (optional)

½ cup sugar-free whipped topping (optional)

1. Spread ¼ cup of the coconut in the bottom of a pie plate and place in the air fryer basket. Set the air fryer to 350°F (177°C) and air fry the coconut while the air fryer preheats, about 5 minutes, until golden brown. Transfer the coconut to a small bowl and set aside for garnish. Brush the pie plate with oil and set aside. 2. In a large bowl, combine the remaining 1 cup shredded coconut, eggs, milk, granulated Swerve, coconut flour, butter, vanilla, and salt. Whisk until smooth. Pour the batter into the prepared pie plate and air fry for 40 to 45 minutes, or until a toothpick inserted into the center of the pie comes out clean. (Check halfway through the baking time and rotate the pan, if necessary, for even baking.) 3. Remove the pie from the air fryer and place on a baking rack to cool completely. Garnish with the reserved toasted coconut and the powdered Swerve or sugar-free whipped topping, if desired. Cover and refrigerate leftover pie for up to 3 days.

Coconut Mixed Berry Crisp

Prep time: 5 minutes | Cook time: 20 minutes | Serves 6

1 tablespoon butter, melted

12 ounces (340 g) mixed berries

⅓ cup granulated Swerve

1 teaspoon pure vanilla extract

½ teaspoon ground cinnamon

¼ teaspoon ground cloves

¼ teaspoon grated nutmeg

½ cup coconut chips, for garnish

1. Preheat the air fryer to 330°F (166°C). Coat a baking pan with melted butter. 2. Put the remaining ingredients except the coconut chips in the prepared baking pan. 3. Bake in the preheated air fryer for 20 minutes. 4. Serve garnished with the coconut chips.

Chocolate Chip Cookie Cake

Prep time: 5 minutes | Cook time: 15 minutes | Serves 8

4 tablespoons salted butter, melted

⅓ cup granular brown erythritol

1 large egg

½ teaspoon vanilla extract

1 cup blanched finely ground almond flour

½ teaspoon baking powder

¼ cup low-carb chocolate chips

In a large bowl, whisk together butter, erythritol, egg, and vanilla. Add flour and baking powder, and stir until combined. 2. Fold in chocolate chips, then spoon batter into an ungreased round nonstick baking dish. 3. Place dish into air fryer basket. Adjust the temperature to 300°F (149°C) and set the timer for 15 minutes. When edges are browned, cookie cake will be done. 4. Slice and serve warm.

Kentucky Chocolate Nut Pie

Prep time: 20 minutes | Cook time: 25 minutes | Serves 8

2 large eggs, beaten

⅓ cup butter, melted

1 cup sugar

½ cup all-purpose flour

1½ cups coarsely chopped

pecans

1 cup milk chocolate chips

2 tablespoons bourbon

1 (9-inch) unbaked piecrust

In a large bowl, stir together the eggs and melted butter. Add the sugar and flour and stir until combined. Stir in the pecans, chocolate chips, and bourbon until well mixed. 2. Using a fork, prick holes in the bottom and sides of the pie crust. Pour the pie filling into the crust. 3. Preheat the air fryer to 350°F (177°C). 4. Cook for 25 minutes, or until a knife inserted into the middle of the pie comes out clean. Let set for 5 minutes before serving.

Chapter 6 Snacks and Appetizers

Shrimp Egg Rolls

Prep time: 15 minutes | Cook time: 10 minutes per batch | Serves 4

1 tablespoon vegetable oil	1 pound (454 g) cooked shrimp, diced
1 tablespoon soy sauce	
½ teaspoon sugar	¼ cup scallions
1 teaspoon sesame oil	8 egg roll wrappers
¼ cup hoisin sauce	Vegetable oil
Freshly ground black pepper, to taste	Duck sauce

1. Preheat a large sauté pan over medium-high heat. Add the oil and when it is hot, add the shrimp, scallions, soy sauce, sugar, sesame oil, hoisin sauce and black pepper. Sauté for a few more minutes. Transfer the mixture to a colander in a bowl to cool. Press or squeeze out any excess water from the filling so that you don't end up with soggy egg rolls. 2. Make the egg rolls: Place the egg roll wrappers on a flat surface with one of the points facing towards you so they look like diamonds. Dividing the filling evenly between the eight wrappers, spoon the mixture onto the center of the egg roll wrappers. Spread the filling across the center of the wrappers from the left corner to the right corner, but leave 2 inches from each corner empty. Brush the empty sides of the wrapper with a little water. Fold the bottom corner of the wrapper tightly up over the filling, trying to avoid making any air pockets. Fold the left corner in toward the center and then the right corner toward the center. It should now look like an envelope. Tightly roll the egg roll from the bottom to the top open corner. Press to seal the egg roll together, brushing with a little extra water if need be. Repeat this technique with all 8 egg rolls. 3. Preheat the air fryer to 370ºF (188ºC). 4. Spray or brush all sides of the egg rolls with vegetable oil. Air fry four egg rolls at a time for 10 minutes, turning them over halfway through the cooking time. 5. Serve hot with duck sauce or your favorite dipping sauce.

Toasted Cauliflower

Prep time: 15 minutes | Cook time: 15 minutes | Makes 5 cups

8 cups small cauliflower florets (about 1¼ pounds / 567 g)	½ teaspoon salt
	½ teaspoon turmeric
3 tablespoons olive oil	½ cup salad sauce, for serving
1 teaspoon garlic powder	1 lemon, for serving

1. Preheat the air fryer to 390ºF (199ºC). 2. In a bowl, combine the cauliflower florets, olive oil, garlic powder, salt, and turmeric and toss to coat. 3. Transfer to the air fryer basket and air fry for 15 minutes, or until the florets are crisp-tender. Shake the basket twice during cooking. 4. Remove from the basket to a plate. Serve warm with sauce and lemon.

Roasted Chickpeas

Prep time: 5 minutes | Cook time: 15 minutes |
Makes about 1 cup

1 (15-ounce / 425-g) can
chickpeas, drained
2 teaspoons curry powder

¼ teaspoon salt
1 tablespoon olive oil

1. Drain chickpeas thoroughly and spread in a single layer on paper towels. Cover with another paper towel and press gently to remove extra moisture. Don't press too hard or you'll crush the chickpeas. 2. Mix curry powder and salt together. 3. Place chickpeas in a medium bowl and sprinkle with seasonings. Stir well to coat. 4. Add olive oil and stir again to distribute oil. 5. Air fry at 390ºF (199ºC) for 15 minutes, stopping to shake basket about halfway through cooking time. 6. Cool completely and store in airtight container.

Honey-Mustard Chicken Wings

Prep time: 10 minutes | Cook time: 24 minutes | Serves 2

2 pounds (907 g) chicken wings
Salt and freshly ground black
pepper, to taste
2 tablespoons butter
¼ cup honey

¼ cup spicy brown mustard
Pinch ground cayenne pepper
2 teaspoons Worcestershire
sauce
½ cup tomato sauce, for serving

1. Prepare the chicken wings by cutting off the wing tips and discarding (or freezing for chicken stock). Divide the drumettes from the wingettes by cutting through the joint. Place the chicken wing pieces in a large bowl. 2. Preheat the air fryer to 400ºF (204ºC). 3. Season the wings with salt and freshly ground black pepper and air fry the wings in two batches for 10 minutes per batch, shaking the basket half way through the cooking process. 4. While the wings are air frying, combine the remaining ingredients in a small saucepan over low heat. 5. When both batches are done, toss all the wings with the honey-mustard sauce and toss them all back into the basket for another 4 minutes to heat through and finish cooking. Give the basket a good shake part way through the cooking process to redistribute the wings. Remove the wings from the air fryer and serve with tomato sauce.

Fried Calamari

Prep time: 20 minutes | Cook time: 8 minutes | Serves 2

½ pound (227 g) calamari bodies and tentacles, bodies cut into ½-inch-wide rings
1 lemon
2 cups all-purpose flour
Kosher salt and freshly ground black pepper, to taste

3 large eggs, lightly beaten
Cooking spray
½ cup mayonnaise
1 teaspoon finely chopped rosemary
1 garlic clove, minced

1. Add the calamari to the brine and let stand in the refrigerator for 20 minutes or up to 2 hours. 2. Grate some of the lemon zest into a large bowl then whisk in the flour and season with salt and pepper. Dip the calamari in the egg, then toss them in the flour mixture until fully coated. Spray the calamari liberally with cooking spray, then transfer half to the air fryer. Air fry at 400ºF (204ºC), shaking the basket halfway into cooking, until the calamari is cooked through and golden brown, about 8 minutes. Transfer to a plate and repeat with the remaining pieces. 3. In a small bowl, whisk together the mayonnaise, rosemary, and garlic. Squeeze half the zested lemon to get 1 tablespoon of juice and stir it into the sauce. Season with salt and pepper. Cut the remaining zested lemon into small wedges and serve alongside the calamari and sauce.

Asian Five-Spice Wings

Prep time: 30 minutes | Cook time: 13 to 15 minutes | Serves 4

2 pounds (907 g) chicken wings
½ cup Asian-style salad dressing

2 tablespoons Chinese five-spice powder
A sprig of dill, for garnish

1. Cut off wing tips and discard or freeze for stock. Cut remaining wing pieces in two at the joint. 2. Place wing pieces in a large sealable plastic bag. Pour in the Asian dressing, seal bag, and massage the marinade into the wings until well coated. Refrigerate for at least an hour. 3. Remove wings from bag, drain off excess marinade, and place wings in air fryer basket. 4. Air fry at 360ºF (182ºC) for 13 to 15 minutes or until juices run clear. About halfway through cooking time, shake the basket or stir wings for more even cooking. 5. Transfer cooked wings to plate in a single layer. Sprinkle half of the Chinese five-spice powder on the wings, turn, and sprinkle other side with remaining seasoning. 6. Serve with a dill.

Cream Cheese Wontons

Prep time: 15 minutes | Cook time: 6 minutes |
Makes 20 wontons

Oil, for spraying

4 ounces (113 g) cream cheese

20 round wonton wrappers

1. Line the air fryer basket with parchment and spray lightly with oil. 2. Pour some water in a small bowl. 3. Lay out a wonton wrapper and place 1 teaspoon of cream cheese in the center. 4. Dip your finger in the water and moisten the edge of the wonton wrapper. Fold in the middle to make a semi-circle and press the edges together and pinch the pleats. 5. Place the wonton in the prepared basket. Repeat with the remaining wrappers and cream cheese. You may need to work in batches, depending on the size of your air fryer. 6. Air fry at 400ºF (204ºC) for 6 minutes, or until golden brown around the edges.

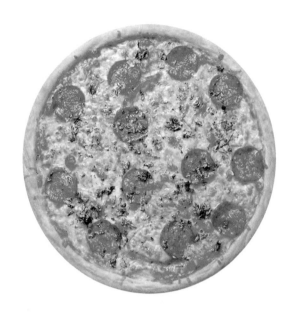

Pepperoni Pizza Dip

Prep time: 10 minutes | Cook time: 10 minutes |
Serves 6

6 ounces (170 g) cream cheese, softened

¾ cup shredded Italian cheese blend

¼ cup sour cream

1½ teaspoons dried Italian seasoning

¼ teaspoon garlic salt

¼ teaspoon onion powder

¾ cup pizza sauce

½ cup sliced miniature pepperoni

1 tablespoon basil leaves, chopped

1. In a small bowl, combine the cream cheese, ¼ cup of the shredded cheese, the sour cream, Italian seasoning, garlic salt, and onion powder. Stir until smooth and the ingredients are well blended. 2. Spread the mixture in a baking pan. Top with the pizza sauce, spreading to the edges. Sprinkle with the remaining ½ cup shredded cheese. Arrange the pepperoni slices on top of the cheese. Top with basil leaves. 3. Place the pan in the air fryer basket. Set the air fryer to 350ºF (177ºC) for 10 minutes, or until the pepperoni is beginning to brown on the edges and the cheese is bubbly and lightly browned. 4. Let stand for 5 minutes before serving.

Sweet Potato Fries with Mayonnaise

Prep time: 5 minutes | Cook time: 20 minutes |
Serves 2 to 3

1 large sweet potato (about 1 pound / 454 g), scrubbed
1 teaspoon vegetable or canola oil
½ lime, for serving
½ avocado, for serving
Salt, to taste

Dipping Sauce:
¼ cup light mayonnaise
½ teaspoon sriracha sauce
1 tablespoon spicy brown mustard
1 tablespoon sweet Thai chili sauce

Preheat the air fryer to 200ºF (93ºC). 2. On a flat work surface, cut the sweet potato into fry-shaped strips about ¼ inch wide and ¼ inch thick. You can use a mandoline to slice the sweet potato quickly and uniformly. 3. In a medium bowl, drizzle the sweet potato strips with the oil and toss well. 4. Transfer to the air fryer basket and air fry for 10 minutes, shaking the basket twice during cooking. 5. Remove the air fryer basket and sprinkle with the salt and toss to coat. 6. Increase the air fryer temperature to 400ºF (204ºC) and air fry for an additional 10 minutes, or until the fries are crispy and tender. Shake the basket a few times during cooking. 7. Meanwhile, whisk together all the ingredients for the sauce in a small bowl. 8. Remove the sweet potato fries from the basket to a plate and serve warm alongside the dipping sauce, lime and avocado. Garnish with cilantro, if desired.

Parmesan French Fries

Prep time: 10 minutes | Cook time: 25 minutes |
Serves 2 to 3

2 to 3 large russet potatoes, peeled and cut into ½-inch sticks
2 teaspoons vegetable or canola oil
¾ cup grated Parmesan cheese

½ teaspoon salt
Freshly ground black pepper, to taste
1 teaspoon fresh chopped parsley
2 tablespoons tomato sauce

1. Bring a large saucepan of salted water to a boil on the stovetop while you peel and cut the potatoes. Blanch the potatoes in the boiling salted water for 4 minutes while you preheat the air fryer to 400ºF (204ºC). Strain the potatoes and rinse them with cold water. Dry them well with a clean kitchen towel. 2. Toss the dried potato sticks gently with the oil and place them in the air fryer basket. Air fry for 25 minutes, shaking the basket a few times while the fries cook to help them brown evenly. 3. Combine the Parmesan cheese, salt and pepper. With 2 minutes left on the air fryer cooking time, sprinkle the fries with the Parmesan cheese mixture. Toss the fries to coat them evenly with the cheese mixture and continue to air fry for the final 2 minutes, until the cheese has melted and just starts to brown. Sprinkle the finished fries with chopped parsley, a little more grated Parmesan cheese if you like, and serve with tomato sauce.

Zucchini Feta Roulades

Prep time: 10 minutes | Cook time: 10 minutes | Serves 6

½ cup feta

1 garlic clove, minced

2 tablespoons fresh basil, minced

1 tablespoon capers, minced

⅛ teaspoon salt

⅛ teaspoon red pepper flakes

1 tablespoon lemon juice

2 medium zucchini

12 toothpicks

1. Preheat the air fryer to 360ºF (182ºC).(If using a grill attachment, make sure it is inside the air fryer during preheating.) 2. In a small bowl, combine the feta, garlic, basil, capers, salt, red pepper flakes, and lemon juice. 3. Slice the zucchini into ⅛-inch strips lengthwise. (Each zucchini should yield around 6 strips.) 4. Spread 1 tablespoon of the cheese filling onto each slice of zucchini, then roll it up and secure it with a toothpick through the middle. 5. Place the zucchini roulades into the air fryer basket in a single layer, making sure that they don't touch each other. 6. Bake or grill in the air fryer for 10 minutes. 7. Remove the zucchini roulades from the air fryer and gently remove the toothpicks before serving.

Ranch Snack Crackers

Prep time: 3 minutes | Cook time: 12 minutes | Serves 6

Oil, for spraying

¼ cup olive oil

2 teaspoons dry ranch seasoning

1 teaspoon chili powder

½ teaspoon dried dill

½ teaspoon granulated garlic

½ teaspoon salt

1 (9-ounce / 255-g) bag crackers

1. Preheat the air fryer to 325ºF (163ºC). Line the air fryer basket with parchment and spray lightly with oil. 2. In a large bowl, mix together the olive oil, ranch seasoning, chili powder, dill, garlic, and salt. Add the crackers and toss until evenly coated. 3. Place the mixture in the prepared basket. 4. Cook for 10 to 12 minutes, shaking or stirring every 3 to 4 minutes, or until crisp and golden brown.

Chicken Meatballs

Prep time: 5 minutes | Cook time: 13 to 20 minutes |
Makes 16 meatballs

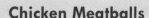

2 teaspoons olive oil	½ teaspoon dried thyme
¼ cup minced onion	½ pound (227 g) ground
2 vanilla wafers, crushed	chicken breast
1 egg white	¼ lemon, for serving

Preheat the air fryer to 370ºF (188ºC). 2. In a baking pan, mix the olive oil and onion. Put the pan in the air fryer. Air fry for 3 to 5 minutes, or until the vegetables are tender. 3. In a medium bowl, mix the cooked vegetables, crushed wafers, egg white, and thyme until well combined 4. Mix in the chicken, gently but thoroughly, until everything is combined. 5. Form the mixture into 16 meatballs and place them in the air fryer basket. Air fry for 10 to 15 minutes, or until the meatballs reach an internal temperature of 165ºF (74ºC) on a meat thermometer. 6. Serve immediately with lemon.

String Bean Fries

Prep time: 15 minutes | Cook time: 5 to 6 minutes |
Serves 4

½ pound (227 g) fresh string	¼ teaspoon salt
beans	¼ teaspoon ground black
2 eggs	pepper
4 teaspoons water	¼ teaspoon dry mustard
½ cup white flour	(optional)
½ cup bread crumbs	Oil for misting or cooking spray
½ cup salad sauce, for serving	

1. Preheat the air fryer to 360ºF (182ºC). 2. Trim stem ends from string beans, wash, and pat dry. 3. In a shallow dish, beat eggs and water together until well blended. 4. Place flour in a second shallow dish. 5. In a third shallow dish, stir together the bread crumbs, salt, pepper, and dry mustard if using. 6. Dip each string bean in egg mixture, flour, egg mixture again, then bread crumbs. 7. When you finish coating all the string beans, open air fryer and place them in basket. 8. Cook for 3 minutes. 9. Stop and mist string beans with oil or cooking spray. 10. Cook for 2 to 3 more minutes or until string beans are crispy and nicely browned. 11. Serve warm with salad sauce.

enough to roll, fold the bottom up over the filling, fold in the sides, and roll the wrapper all the way up. (Basically, make a tiny burrito.) 4. Repeat step 3 to make the remaining spring rolls until you have the number of spring rolls you want to cook right now (and the amount that will fit in the air fryer basket in a single layer without them touching each other). Refrigerate any leftover filling in an airtight container for about 1 week. 5. Insert the crisper plate into the basket and the basket into the unit. Preheat the unit by selecting AIR FRY, setting the temperature to 390°F (199°C), and setting the time to 3 minutes. Select START/STOP to begin. 6. Once the unit is preheated, spray the crisper plate and the basket with cooking oil. Place the spring rolls into the basket, leaving a little room between them so they don't stick to each other. Spray the top of each spring roll with cooking oil. 7. Select AIR FRY, set the temperature to 390°F (199°C), and set the time to 9 minutes. Select START/STOP to begin. 8. When the cooking is complete, the egg rolls should be crisp-ish and lightly browned. Garnish with parsley leaves and serve immediately with shrimps.

Zucchini Fries with Roasted Garlic Aïoli

Prep time: 20 minutes | Cook time: 12 minutes | Serves 4

1 tablespoon vegetable oil	Zucchini Fries:
½ head green or savoy cabbage, finely shredded	½ cup flour
Roasted Garlic Aïoli:	2 eggs, beaten
1 teaspoon roasted garlic	1 cup seasoned bread crumbs
½ cup mayonnaise	Salt and pepper, to taste
2 tablespoons olive oil	1 large zucchini, cut into ½-inch
Juice of ½ lemon	sticks
Salt and pepper, to taste	Olive oil

Make the aïoli: Combine the roasted garlic, mayonnaise, olive oil and lemon juice in a bowl and whisk well. Season the aïoli with salt and pepper to taste. 2. Prepare the zucchini fries. Create a dredging station with three shallow dishes. Place the flour in the first shallow dish and season well with salt and freshly ground black pepper. Put the beaten eggs in the second shallow dish. In the third shallow dish, combine the bread crumbs, salt and pepper. Dredge the zucchini sticks, coating with flour first, then dipping them into the eggs to coat, and finally tossing in bread crumbs. Shake the dish with the bread crumbs and pat the crumbs onto the zucchini sticks gently with your hands so they stick evenly. 3. Place the zucchini fries on a flat surface and let them sit at least 10 minutes before air frying to let them dry out a little. Preheat the air fryer to 400°F (204°C). 4. Spray the zucchini sticks with olive oil, and place them into the air fryer basket. You can air fry the zucchini in two layers, placing the second layer in the opposite direction to the first. Air fry for 12 minutes turning and rotating the fries halfway through the cooking time. Spray with additional oil when you turn them over. 5. Serve zucchini fries warm with the roasted garlic aïoli.

Classic Spring Rolls

Prep time: 10 minutes | Cook time: 9 minutes | Makes 16 spring rolls

4 teaspoons toasted sesame oil	1 cup grated carrot
6 medium garlic cloves, minced or pressed	½ teaspoon sea salt
	16 rice paper wrappers
1 tablespoon grated peeled fresh ginger	Cooking oil spray (sunflower, safflower, or refined coconut)
2 cups thinly sliced shiitake mushrooms	2 shrimps, for serving (optional)
	3 parsley leaves, for garnish
4 cups chopped green cabbage	(optional)

1. Place a wok or sauté pan over medium heat until hot. 2. Add the sesame oil, garlic, ginger, mushrooms, cabbage, carrot, and salt. Cook for 3 to 4 minutes, stirring often, until the cabbage is lightly wilted. Remove the pan from the heat. 3. Gently run a rice paper under water. Lay it on a flat nonabsorbent surface. Place about ¼ cup of the cabbage filling in the middle. Once the wrapper is soft

Garlic-Roasted Tomatoes and Olives

Prep time: 5 minutes | Cook time: 20 minutes | Serves 6

2 cups cherry tomatoes	1 tablespoon fresh basil, minced
4 garlic cloves, roughly chopped	1 tablespoon fresh oregano, minced
½ red onion, roughly chopped	2 tablespoons olive oil
1 cup black olives	¼ to ½ teaspoon salt
1 cup green olives	

1. Preheat the air fryer to 380°F(193°C). 2. In a large bowl, combine all of the ingredients and toss together so that the tomatoes and olives are coated well with the olive oil and herbs. 3. Pour the mixture into the air fryer basket, and roast for 10 minutes. Stir the mixture well, then continue roasting for an additional 10 minutes. 4. Remove from the air fryer, transfer to a serving bowl, and enjoy.

Rosemary-Garlic Shoestring Fries

Prep time: 5 minutes | Cook time: 18 minutes | Serves 2

1 large russet potato (about 12 ounces / 340 g), scrubbed clean, and julienned	rosemary
	Kosher salt and freshly ground black pepper, to taste
1 tablespoon vegetable oil	1 garlic clove, thinly sliced
Leaves from 1 sprig fresh	Flaky sea salt, for serving

1. Preheat the air fryer to 400°F (204°C). 2. Place the julienned potatoes in a large colander and rinse under cold running water until the water runs clear. Spread the potatoes out on a double-thick layer of paper towels and pat dry. 3. In a large bowl, combine the potatoes, oil, and rosemary. Season with kosher salt and pepper and toss to coat evenly. Place the potatoes in the air fryer and air fry for 18 minutes, shaking the basket every 5 minutes and adding the garlic in the last 5 minutes of cooking, or until the fries are golden brown and crisp. 4. Transfer the fries to a plate and sprinkle with flaky sea salt while they're hot. Serve immediately.

Cheesy Zucchini Tots

Prep time: 15 minutes | Cook time: 6 minutes | Serves 8

2 medium zucchini (about 12 ounces / 340 g), shredded	½ cup panko bread crumbs
	¼ teaspoon black pepper
1 large egg, whisked	1 clove garlic, minced
½ cup grated pecorino romano cheese	Cooking spray

1. Using your hands, squeeze out as much liquid from the zucchini as possible. In a large bowl, mix the zucchini with the remaining ingredients except the oil until well incorporated. 2. Make the zucchini tots: Use a spoon or cookie scoop to place tablespoonfuls of the zucchini mixture onto a lightly floured cutting board and form into 1-inch logs. 3. Preheat air fryer to 375°F (191°C). Spritz the air fryer basket with cooking spray. 4. Place the tots in the basket. You may need to cook in batches to avoid overcrowding. 5. Air fry for 6 minutes until golden brown. 6. Remove from the basket to a serving plate and repeat with the remaining zucchini tots. 7. Serve immediately.

Artichoke and Olive Pita Flatbread

Prep time: 5 minutes | Cook time: 10 minutes | Serves 4

2 whole wheat pitas	¼ cup Kalamata olives
2 tablespoons olive oil, divided	¼ cup shredded Parmesan
2 garlic cloves, minced	¼ cup crumbled feta
¼ teaspoon salt	Chopped fresh parsley, for garnish (optional)
½ cup canned artichoke hearts, sliced	

1. Preheat the air fryer to 380°F(193°C). 2. Brush each pita with 1 tablespoon olive oil, then sprinkle the minced garlic and salt over the top. 3. Distribute the artichoke hearts, olives, and cheeses evenly between the two pitas, and place both into the air fryer to bake for 10 minutes. 4. Remove the pitas and cut them into 4 pieces each before serving. Sprinkle parsley over the top, if desired.

Lebanese Muhammara

Prep time: 15 minutes | Cook time: 15 minutes | Serves 6

2 large red bell peppers	1 teaspoon ground cumin
¼ cup plus 2 tablespoons extra-virgin olive oil	1 teaspoon kosher salt
	1 teaspoon red pepper flakes
1 cup walnut halves	Raw vegetables (such as cucumber, carrots, zucchini slices, or cauliflower) or toasted pita chips, for serving
1 tablespoon agave nectar or honey	
1 teaspoon fresh lemon juice	

1. Drizzle the peppers with 2 tablespoons of the olive oil and place in the air fryer basket. Set the air fryer to 400°F (204°C) for 10 minutes. 2. Add the walnuts to the basket, arranging them around the peppers. Set the air fryer to 400°F (204°C) for 5 minutes. 3. Remove the peppers, seal in a resealable plastic bag, and let rest for 5 to 10 minutes. Transfer the walnuts to a plate and set aside to cool. 4. Place the softened peppers, walnuts, agave, lemon juice, cumin, salt, and ½ teaspoon of the pepper flakes in a food processor and purée until smooth. 5. Transfer the dip to a serving bowl and make an indentation in the middle. Pour the remaining ¼ cup olive oil into the indentation. Garnish the dip with the remaining ½ teaspoon pepper flakes. 6. Serve with vegetables or toasted pita chips.

Crunchy Tex-Mex Tortilla Chips

Prep time: 5 minutes | Cook time: 5 minutes | Serves 4

Olive oil	½ teaspoon paprika
½ teaspoon salt	Pinch cayenne pepper
½ teaspoon ground cumin	8 (6-inch) corn tortillas, each
½ teaspoon chili powder	cut into 6 wedges

1. Spray fryer basket lightly with olive oil. 2. In a small bowl, combine the salt, cumin, chili powder, paprika, and cayenne pepper. 3. Place the tortilla wedges in the air fryer basket in a single layer. Spray the tortillas lightly with oil and sprinkle with some of the seasoning mixture. You will need to cook the tortillas in batches. 4. Air fry at 375ºF (191ºC) for 2 to 3 minutes. Shake the basket and cook until the chips are light brown and crispy, an additional 2 to 3 minutes. Watch the chips closely so they do not burn.

Black Bean Corn Dip

Prep time: 10 minutes | Cook time: 10 minutes | Serves 4

½ (15-ounce / 425-g) can black beans, drained and rinsed	¼ cup shredded reduced-fat Cheddar cheese
½ (15-ounce / 425-g) can corn, drained and rinsed	½ teaspoon ground cumin
¼ cup chunky salsa	½ teaspoon paprika
2 ounces (57 g) reduced-fat cream cheese, softened	Salt and freshly ground black pepper, to taste

1. Preheat the air fryer to 325ºF (163ºC). 2. In a medium bowl, mix together the black beans, corn, salsa, cream cheese, Cheddar cheese, cumin, and paprika. Season with salt and pepper and stir until well combined. 3. Spoon the mixture into a baking dish. 4. Place baking dish in the air fryer basket and bake until heated through, about 10 minutes. 5. Serve hot.

Vegetable Pot Stickers

Prep time: 12 minutes | Cook time: 11 to 18 minutes | Makes 12 pot stickers

1 cup shredded red cabbage	2 garlic cloves, minced
¼ cup chopped button mushrooms	2 teaspoons grated fresh ginger
¼ cup grated carrot	12 gyoza/pot sticker wrappers
2 tablespoons minced onion	2½ teaspoons olive oil, divided

1. In a baking pan, combine the red cabbage, mushrooms, carrot, onion, garlic, and ginger. Add 1 tablespoon of water. Place in the air fryer and air fry at 370ºF (188ºC) for 3 to 6 minutes, until the vegetables are crisp-tender. Drain and set aside. 2. Working one at a time, place the pot sticker wrappers on a work surface. Top each wrapper with a scant 1 tablespoon of the filling. Fold half of the wrapper over the other half to form a half circle. Dab one edge with water and press both edges together. 3. To another pan, add 1¼ teaspoons of olive oil. Put half of the pot stickers, seam-side up, in the pan. Air fry for 5 minutes, or until the bottoms are light golden brown. Add 1 tablespoon of water and return the pan to the air fryer. 4. Air fry for 4 to 6 minutes more, or until hot. Repeat with the remaining pot stickers, remaining 1¼ teaspoons of oil, and another tablespoon of water. Serve immediately.

Fried Artichoke Hearts

Prep time: 10 minutes | Cook time: 12 minutes | Serves 10

Oil, for spraying	1 cup panko bread crumbs
3 (14-ounce / 397-g) cans quartered artichokes, drained and patted dry	⅓ cup grated Parmesan cheese
	Salt and freshly ground black pepper, to taste
½ cup mayonnaise	

1. Line the air fryer basket with parchment and spray lightly with oil. 2. Place the artichokes on a plate. Put the mayonnaise and bread crumbs in separate bowls. 3. Working one at a time, dredge each artichoke piece in the mayonnaise, then in the bread crumbs to cover. 4. Place the artichokes in the prepared basket. You may need to work in batches, depending on the size of your air fryer. 5. Air fry at 370ºF (188ºC) for 10 to 12 minutes, or until crispy and golden brown. 6. Sprinkle with the Parmesan cheese and season with salt and black pepper. Serve immediately.

Spiced Nuts

Prep time: 5 minutes | Cook time: 25 minutes | Makes 3 cups

1 egg white, lightly beaten	¼ teaspoon ground allspice
¼ cup sugar	Pinch ground cayenne pepper
1 teaspoon salt	1 cup pecan halves
½ teaspoon ground cinnamon	1 cup cashews
¼ teaspoon ground cloves	1 cup almonds

Combine the egg white with the sugar and spices in a bowl. 2. Preheat the air fryer to 300ºF (149ºC). 3. Spray or brush the air fryer basket with vegetable oil. Toss the nuts together in the spiced egg white and transfer the nuts to the air fryer basket. 4. Air fry for 25 minutes, stirring the nuts in the basket a few times during the cooking process. Taste the nuts (carefully because they will be very hot) to see if they are crunchy and nicely toasted. Air fry for a few more minutes if necessary. 5. Serve warm or cool to room temperature and store in an airtight container for up to two weeks.

Crispy Breaded Beef Cubes

Prep time: 10 minutes | Cook time: 12 to 16 minutes | Serves 4

1 pound (454 g) sirloin tip, cut into 1-inch cubes	1½ cups soft bread crumbs
1 cup cheese pasta sauce	2 tablespoons olive oil
	½ teaspoon dried marjoram

Preheat the air fryer to 360ºF (182ºC). 2. In a medium bowl, toss the beef with the pasta sauce to coat. 3. In a shallow bowl, combine the bread crumbs, oil, and marjoram, and mix well. Drop the beef cubes, one at a time, into the bread crumb mixture to coat thoroughly. 4. Air fry the beef in two batches for 6 to 8 minutes, shaking the basket once during cooking time, until the beef is at least 145ºF (63ºC) and the outside is crisp and brown. 5. Serve hot.

Air Fried Pot Stickers

Prep time: 10 minutes | Cook time: 18 to 20 minutes | Makes 30 pot stickers

½ cup finely chopped cabbage	2 teaspoons low-sodium soy sauce
¼ cup finely chopped red bell pepper	30 wonton wrappers
2 green onions, finely chopped	1 tablespoon water, for brushing the wrappers
1 egg, beaten	
2 tablespoons cocktail sauce	

1. Preheat the air fryer to 360ºF (182ºC). 2. In a small bowl, combine the cabbage, pepper, green onions, egg, cocktail sauce, and soy sauce, and mix well. 3. Put about 1 teaspoon of the mixture in the center of each wonton wrapper. Fold the wrapper in half, covering the filling; dampen the edges with water, and seal. You can crimp the edges of the wrapper with your fingers so they look like the pot stickers you get in restaurants. Brush them with water. 4. Place the pot stickers in the air fryer basket and air fry in 2 batches for 9 to 10 minutes, or until the pot stickers are hot and the bottoms are lightly browned. 5. Serve hot.

Greek Street Tacos

Prep time: 10 minutes | Cook time: 3 minutes | Makes 8 small tacos

8 small flour tortillas (4-inch diameter)	cheese
8 tablespoons hummus	4 tablespoons chopped kalamata or other olives (optional)
4 tablespoons crumbled feta	Olive oil for misting

1. Place 1 tablespoon of hummus or tapenade in the center of each tortilla. Top with 1 teaspoon of feta crumbles and 1 teaspoon of chopped olives, if using. 2. Using your finger or a small spoon, moisten the edges of the tortilla all around with water. 3. Fold tortilla over to make a half-moon shape. Press center gently. Then press the edges firmly to seal in the filling. 4. Mist both sides with olive oil. 5. Place in air fryer basket very close but try not to overlap. 6. Air fry at 390ºF (199ºC) for 3 minutes, just until lightly browned and crispy.

Eggplant Fries

Prep time: 10 minutes | Cook time: 7 to 8 minutes per batch | Serves 4

1 medium eggplant	1 cup crushed panko bread crumbs
1 teaspoon ground coriander	
1 teaspoon cumin	1 large egg
1 teaspoon garlic powder	2 tablespoons water
½ teaspoon salt	Oil for misting or cooking spray

1. Peel and cut the eggplant into fat fries, ⅜- to ½-inch thick. 2. Preheat the air fryer to 390ºF (199ºC). 3. In a small cup, mix together the coriander, cumin, garlic, and salt. 4. Combine 1 teaspoon of the seasoning mix and panko crumbs in a shallow dish. 5. Place eggplant fries in a large bowl, sprinkle with remaining seasoning, and stir well to combine. 6. Beat eggs and water together and pour over eggplant fries. Stir to coat. 7. Remove eggplant from egg wash, shaking off excess, and roll in panko crumbs. 8. Spray with oil. 9. Place half of the fries in air fryer basket. You should have only a single layer, but it's fine if they overlap a little. 10. Cook for 5 minutes. Shake basket, mist lightly with oil, and cook 2 to 3 minutes longer, until browned and crispy. 11. Repeat step 10 to cook remaining eggplant.

Greens Chips with Curried Yogurt Sauce

Prep time: 10 minutes | Cook time: 5 to 6 minutes | Serves 4

1 cup low-fat Greek yogurt	leaves cut into 2- to 3-inch pieces
1 tablespoon freshly squeezed lemon juice	½ bunch chard, stemmed, ribs removed and discarded, leaves cut into 2- to 3-inch pieces
1 tablespoon curry powder	
½ bunch curly kale, stemmed, ribs removed and discarded,	1½ teaspoons olive oil

1. In a small bowl, stir together the yogurt, lemon juice, and curry powder. Set aside. 2. In a large bowl, toss the kale and chard with the olive oil, working the oil into the leaves with your hands. This helps break up the fibers in the leaves so the chips are tender. 3. Air fry the greens in batches at 390ºF (199ºC) for 5 to 6 minutes, until crisp, shaking the basket once during cooking. Serve with the yogurt sauce.

Shishito Peppers with Herb Dressing

Prep time: 10 minutes | Cook time: 6 minutes | Serves 2 to 4

6 ounces (170 g) shishito peppers
1 tablespoon vegetable oil
Kosher salt and freshly ground black pepper, to taste
½ cup mayonnaise
2 tablespoons finely chopped fresh basil leaves
2 tablespoons finely chopped

fresh flat-leaf parsley
1 tablespoon finely chopped fresh tarragon
1 tablespoon finely chopped fresh chives
Finely grated zest of ½ lemon
1 tablespoon fresh lemon juice
Flaky sea salt, for serving

Preheat the air fryer to 400ºF (204ºC). 2. In a bowl, toss together the shishitos and oil to evenly coat and season with kosher salt and black pepper. Transfer to the air fryer and air fry for 6 minutes, shaking the basket halfway through, or until the shishitos are blistered and lightly charred. 3. Meanwhile, in a small bowl, whisk together the mayonnaise, basil, parsley, tarragon, chives, lemon zest, and lemon juice. 4. Pile the peppers on a plate, sprinkle with flaky sea salt, and serve hot with the dressing.

Mexican Potato Skins

Prep time: 10 minutes | Cook time: 55 minutes | Serves 6

Olive oil
6 medium russet potatoes, scrubbed
Salt and freshly ground black pepper, to taste
1 cup fat-free refried black

beans
1 tablespoon taco seasoning
½ cup salsa
¾ cup reduced-fat shredded Cheddar cheese

1. Spray the air fryer basket lightly with olive oil. 2. Spray the potatoes lightly with oil and season with salt and pepper. Pierce each potato a few times with a fork. 3. Place the potatoes in the air fryer basket. Air fry at 400ºF (204ºC) until fork-tender, 30 to 40 minutes. The cooking time will depend on the size of the potatoes. You can cook the potatoes in the microwave or a standard oven, but they won't get the same lovely crispy skin they will get in the air fryer. 4. While the potatoes are cooking, in a small bowl, mix together the beans and taco seasoning. Set aside until the potatoes are cool enough to handle. 5. Cut each potato in half lengthwise. Scoop out most of the insides, leaving about ¼ inch in the skins so the potato skins hold their shape. 6. Season the insides of the potato skins with salt and black pepper. Lightly spray the insides of the potato skins with oil. You may need to cook them in batches. 7. Place them into the air fryer basket, skin-side down, and air fry until crisp and golden, 8 to 10 minutes. 8. Transfer the skins to a work surface and spoon ½ tablespoon of seasoned refried black beans into each one. Top each with 2 teaspoons salsa and 1 tablespoon shredded Cheddar cheese. 9. Place filled potato skins in the air fryer basket in a single layer. Lightly spray with oil. 10. Air fry until the cheese is melted and bubbly, 2 to 3 minutes.

Crispy Green Bean Fries with Lemon-Yogurt Sauce

Prep time: 5 minutes | Cook time: 5 minutes | Serves 4

Green Beans:
1 egg
2 tablespoons water
1 tablespoon whole wheat flour
¼ teaspoon paprika
½ teaspoon garlic powder
½ teaspoon salt
¼ cup whole wheat bread crumbs

½ pound (227 g) whole green beans
Lemon-Yogurt Sauce:
½ cup nonfat plain Greek yogurt
1 tablespoon lemon juice
¼ teaspoon salt
⅛ teaspoon cayenne pepper

Make the Green Beans: 1. Preheat the air fryer to 380°F(193°C). 2. In a medium shallow bowl, beat together the egg and water until frothy. 3. In a separate medium shallow bowl, whisk together the flour, paprika, garlic powder, and salt, then mix in the bread crumbs. 4. Spray the bottom of the air fryer with cooking spray. 5. Dip each green bean into the egg mixture, then into the bread crumb mixture, coating the outside with the crumbs. Place the green beans in a single layer in the bottom of the air fryer basket. 6. Fry in the air fryer for 5 minutes, or until the breading is golden brown. Make the Lemon-Yogurt Sauce: 7. In a small bowl, combine the yogurt, lemon juice, salt, and cayenne. 8. Serve the green bean fries alongside the lemon-yogurt sauce as a snack or appetizer.

Veggie Salmon Nachos

Prep time: 10 minutes | Cook time: 9 to 12 minutes | Serves 6

2 ounces (57 g) baked no-salt corn tortilla chips
1 (5-ounce / 142-g) baked salmon fillet, flaked
½ cup canned low-sodium black beans, rinsed and drained

1 red bell pepper, chopped
½ cup grated carrot
1 jalapeño pepper, minced
⅓ cup shredded low-sodium low-fat Swiss cheese
1 tomato, chopped

Preheat the air fryer to 360ºF (182ºC). 2. In a baking pan, layer the tortilla chips. Top with the salmon, black beans, red bell pepper, carrot, jalapeño, and Swiss cheese. 3. Bake in the air fryer for 9 to 12 minutes, or until the cheese is melted and starts to brown. 4. Top with the tomato and serve.

Buffalo Bites

Prep time: 15 minutes | Cook time: 11 to 12 minutes
per batch | Makes 16 meatballs

1½ cups cooked jasmine or
sushi rice
¼ teaspoon salt
1 pound (454 g) ground chicken
8 tablespoons buffalo wing

sauce
2 ounces (57 g) Gruyère cheese,
cut into 16 cubes
1 tablespoon maple syrup

1. Mix 4 tablespoons buffalo wing sauce into all the ground chicken. 2. Shape chicken into a log and divide into 16 equal portions. 3. With slightly damp hands, mold each chicken portion around a cube of cheese and shape into a firm ball. When you have shaped 8 meatballs, place them in air fryer basket. 4. Air fry at 390°F (199°C) for approximately 5 minutes. Shake basket, reduce temperature to 360°F (182°C), and cook for 5 to 6 minutes longer. 5. While the first batch is cooking, shape remaining chicken and cheese into 8 more meatballs. 6. Repeat step 4 to cook second batch of meatballs. 7. In a medium bowl, mix the remaining 4 tablespoons of buffalo wing sauce with the maple syrup. Add all the cooked meatballs and toss to coat. 8. Place meatballs back into air fryer basket and air fry at 390°F (199°C) for 2 to 3 minutes to set the glaze. Skewer each with a toothpick and serve.

Hush Puppies

Prep time: 45 minutes | Cook time: 10 minutes |
Serves 12

1 cup self-rising yellow
cornmeal
½ cup all-purpose flour
1 teaspoon sugar
1 teaspoon salt
1 teaspoon freshly ground black
pepper

1 large egg
⅓ cup canned creamed corn
1 cup minced onion
2 teaspoons minced jalapeño
pepper
2 tablespoons olive oil, divided

Thoroughly combine the cornmeal, flour, sugar, salt, and pepper in a large bowl. 2. Whisk together the egg and corn in a small bowl. Pour the egg mixture into the bowl of cornmeal mixture and stir to combine. Stir in the minced onion and jalapeño. Cover the bowl with plastic wrap and place in the refrigerator for 30 minutes. 3. Preheat the air fryer to 375°F (191°C). Line the air fryer basket with parchment paper and lightly brush it with 1 tablespoon of olive oil. 4. Scoop out the cornmeal mixture and form into 24 balls, about 1 inch. 5. Arrange the balls in the parchment paper-lined basket, leaving space between each ball. 6. Air fry in batches for 5 minutes. Shake the basket and brush the balls with the remaining 1 tablespoon of olive oil. Continue cooking for 5 minutes until golden brown. 7. Remove the balls (hush puppies) from the basket and serve on a plate.

Old Bay Chicken Wings

Prep time: 10 minutes | Cook time: 12 to 15 minutes
| Serves 4

2 tablespoons Old Bay
seasoning
2 teaspoons baking powder
2 teaspoons salt

2 pounds (907 g) chicken
wings, patted dry
Cooking spray

1. Preheat the air fryer to 400°F (204°C). Lightly spray the air fryer basket with cooking spray. 2. Combine the Old Bay seasoning, baking powder, and salt in a large zip-top plastic bag. Add the chicken wings, seal, and shake until the wings are thoroughly coated in the seasoning mixture. 3. Lay the chicken wings in the air fryer basket in a single layer and lightly mist with cooking spray. You may need to work in batches to avoid overcrowding. 4. Air fry for 12 to 15 minutes, flipping the wings halfway through, or until the wings are lightly browned and the internal temperature reaches at least 165°F (74°C) on a meat thermometer. 5. Remove from the basket to a plate and repeat with the remaining chicken wings. 6. Serve hot.

Grilled Ham and Cheese on Raisin Bread

Prep time: 5 minutes | Cook time: 10 minutes | Serves 1

2 slices raisin bread
2 tablespoons butter, softened
2 teaspoons honey mustard
3 slices thinly sliced honey ham

(about 3 ounces / 85 g)
4 slices Muenster cheese (about
3 ounces / 85 g)
2 toothpicks

Preheat the air fryer to 370°F (188°C). 2. Spread the softened butter on one side of both slices of raisin bread and place the bread, buttered side down on the counter. Spread the honey mustard on the other side of each slice of bread. Layer 2 slices of cheese, the ham and the remaining 2 slices of cheese on one slice of bread and top with the other slice of bread. Remember to leave the buttered side of the bread on the outside. 3. Transfer the sandwich to the air fryer basket and secure the sandwich with toothpicks. 4. Air fry for 5 minutes. Flip the sandwich over, remove the toothpicks and air fry for another 5 minutes. Cut the sandwich in half and enjoy!

Onion Pakoras

Prep time: 30 minutes | Cook time: 10 minutes per batch | Serves 2

2 medium yellow or white onions, sliced (2 cups)

½ cup chopped fresh cilantro

2 tablespoons vegetable oil

1 tablespoon chickpea flour

1 tablespoon rice flour, or 2 tablespoons chickpea flour

1 teaspoon ground turmeric

1 teaspoon cumin seeds

1 teaspoon kosher salt

½ teaspoon cayenne pepper

Vegetable oil spray

1. In a large bowl, combine the onions, cilantro, oil, chickpea flour, rice flour, turmeric, cumin seeds, salt, and cayenne. Stir to combine. Cover and let stand for 30 minutes or up to overnight. (This allows the onions to release moisture, creating a batter.) Mix well before using. 2. Spray the air fryer basket generously with vegetable oil spray. Drop half of the batter in 6 heaping tablespoons into the basket. Set the air fryer to 350ºF (177ºC) for 8 minutes. Carefully turn the pakoras over and spray with oil spray. Set the air fryer for 2 minutes, or until the batter is cooked through and crisp. 3. Repeat with remaining batter to make 6 more pakoras, checking at 6 minutes for doneness. Serve hot.

Poutine with Waffle Fries

Prep time: 10 minutes | Cook time: 15 to 17 minutes | Serves 4

2 cups frozen waffle cut fries

2 teaspoons olive oil

1 red bell pepper, chopped

2 green onions, sliced

1 cup shredded Swiss cheese

½ cup bottled chicken gravy

Preheat the air fryer to 380ºF (193ºC). 2. Toss the waffle fries with the olive oil and place in the air fryer basket. Air fry for 10 to 12 minutes, or until the fries are crisp and light golden brown, shaking the basket halfway through the cooking time. 3. Transfer the fries to a baking pan and top with the pepper, green onions, and cheese. Air fry for 3 minutes, or until the vegetables are crisp and tender. 4. Remove the pan from the air fryer and drizzle the gravy over the fries. Air fry for 2 minutes, or until the gravy is hot. 5. Serve immediately.

Appendix 1 Measurement Conversion Chart

MEASUREMENT CONVERSION CHART

VOLUME EQUIVALENTS(DRY)

US STANDARD	METRIC (APPROXIMATE)
1/8 teaspoon	0.5 mL
1/4 teaspoon	1 mL
1/2 teaspoon	2 mL
3/4 teaspoon	4 mL
1 teaspoon	5 mL
1 tablespoon	15 mL
1/4 cup	59 mL
1/2 cup	118 mL
3/4 cup	177 mL
1 cup	235 mL
2 cups	475 mL
3 cups	700 mL
4 cups	1 L

WEIGHT EQUIVALENTS

US STANDARD	METRIC (APPROXIMATE)
1 ounce	28 g
2 ounces	57 g
5 ounces	142 g
10 ounces	284 g
15 ounces	425 g
16 ounces (1 pound)	455 g
1.5 pounds	680 g
2 pounds	907 g

VOLUME EQUIVALENTS(LIQUID)

US STANDARD	US STANDARD (OUNCES)	METRIC (APPROXIMATE)
2 tablespoons	1 fl.oz.	30 mL
1/4 cup	2 fl.oz.	60 mL
1/2 cup	4 fl.oz.	120 mL
1 cup	8 fl.oz.	240 mL
1 1/2 cup	12 fl.oz.	355 mL
2 cups or 1 pint	16 fl.oz.	475 mL
4 cups or 1 quart	32 fl.oz.	1 L
1 gallon	128 fl.oz.	4 L

TEMPERATURES EQUIVALENTS

FAHRENHEIT(F)	CELSIUS(C) (APPROXIMATE)
225 °F	107 °C
250 °F	120 °C
275 °F	135 °C
300 °F	150 °C
325 °F	160 °C
350 °F	180 °C
375 °F	190 °C
400 °F	205 °C
425 °F	220 °C
450 °F	235 °C
475 °F	245 °C
500 °F	260 °C

Air Fryer Cooking Chart

Beef

Item	Temp (°F)	Time (mins)	Item	Temp (°F)	Time (mins)
Beef Eye Round Roast (4 lbs.)	400 °F	45 to 55	Meatballs (1-inch)	370 °F	7
Burger Patty (4 oz.)	370 °F	16 to 20	Meatballs (3-inch)	380 °F	10
Filet Mignon (8 oz.)	400 °F	18	Ribeye, bone-in (1-inch, 8 oz)	400 °F	10 to 15
Flank Steak (1.5 lbs.)	400 °F	12	Sirloin steaks (1-inch, 12 oz)	400 °F	9 to 14
Flank Steak (2 lbs.)	400 °F	20 to 28			

Chicken

Item	Temp (°F)	Time (mins)	Item	Temp (°F)	Time (mins)
Breasts, bone in (1 ¼ lb.)	370 °F	25	Legs, bone-in (1 ¾ lb.)	380 °F	30
Breasts, boneless (4 oz)	380 °F	12	Thighs, boneless (1 ½ lb.)	380 °F	18 to 20
Drumsticks (2 ½ lb.)	370 °F	20	Wings (2 lb.)	400 °F	12
Game Hen (halved 2 lb.)	390 °F	20	Whole Chicken	360 °F	75
Thighs, bone-in (2 lb.)	380 °F	22	Tenders	360 °F	8 to 10

Pork & Lamb

Item	Temp (°F)	Time (mins)	Item	Temp (°F)	Time (mins)
Bacon (regular)	400 °F	5 to 7	Pork Tenderloin	370 °F	15
Bacon (thick cut)	400 °F	6 to 10	Sausages	380 °F	15
Pork Loin (2 lb.)	360 °F	55	Lamb Loin Chops (1-inch thick)	400 °F	8 to 12
Pork Chops, bone in (1-inch, 6.5 oz)	400 °F	12	Rack of Lamb (1.5 – 2 lb.)	380 °F	22

Fish & Seafood

Item	Temp (°F)	Time (mins)	Item	Temp (°F)	Time (mins)
Calamari (8 oz)	400 °F	4	Tuna Steak	400 °F	7 to 10
Fish Fillet (1-inch, 8 oz)	400 °F	10	Scallops	400 °F	5 to 7
Salmon, fillet (6 oz)	380 °F	12	Shrimp	400 °F	5
Swordfish steak	400 °F	10			

Air Fryer Cooking Chart

Vegetables					
INGREDIENT	**AMOUNT**	**PREPARATION**	**OIL**	**TEMP**	**COOK TIME**
Asparagus	2 bunches	Cut in half, trim stems	2Tbsp	420°F	12-15 mins
Beets	1½ lbs	Peel, cut in ½-inch cubes	1Tbsp	390°F	28-30 mins
Bell peppers (for roasting)	4 peppers	Cut in quarters, remove seeds	1Tbsp	400°F	15-20 mins
Broccoli	1 large head	Cut in 1-2-inch florets	1Tbsp	400°F	15-20 mins
Brussels sprouts	1 lb	Cut in half, remove stems	1Tbsp	425°F	15-20 mins
Carrots	1 lb	Peel, cut in ¼-inch rounds	1Tbsp	425°F	10-15 mins
Cauliflower	1 head	Cut in 1-2-inch florets	2Tbsp	400°F	20-22 mins
Corn on the cob	7 ears	Whole ears, remove husks	1Tbsp	400°F	14-17 mins
Green beans	1 bag(12 oz)	Trim	1Tbsp	420°F	18-20 mins
Kale (for chips)	4 oz	Tear into pieces, remove stems	None	325°F	5-8 mins
Mushrooms	16 oz	Rinse, slice thinly	1Tbsp	390°F	25-30 mins
Potatoes, russet	1½ lbs	Cut in 1-inch wedges	1Tbsp	390°F	25-30 mins
Potatoes, russet	1 lb	Hand-cut fries, soak 30 mins in cold water, then pat dry	½ -3Tbsp	400°F	25-28 mins
Potatoes, sweet	1 lb	Hand-cut fries, soak 30 mins in cold water, then pat dry	1Tbsp	400°F	25-28 mins
Zucchini	1 lb	Cut in eighths lengthwise, then cut in half	1Tbsp	400°F	15-20 mins

Made in United States
Troutdale, OR
01/18/2024